Through the Gates: A Practice for Counting the Omer

Susan Windle

with photographs by Matthew van der Giessen

Dearest Matthew ~
My cup overflows ...
Thank you from the depths
for this exquisite dance!
Much love and many blessings ~
Susan/Shoshana Ceciel
5/13/2012

Through the Gates: A Practice for Counting the Omer
©2012, 2013 by Susan Windle

ISBN-13: 978-1482610161

Photographs, including cover image, ©2012, 2013 by
Matthew van der Giessen.

www.susanwindle.com

susan@susanwindle.com

Acknowledgments

In addition to the many thanks in my Afterword, I want to bow to my friend Pat Squire for such substantial support of this project. I am continually blessed with your friendship. And Shefa, you created the container into which the original letters were poured, and for so much more, I thank you. Thanks also to Phyllis Berman and Arthur Waskow for your encouragement of my writings and for standing at the threshold of Judaism for me in your warm and welcoming way. Thanks to Saadi (Neil Douglas-Klotz) for opening me to the wisdom of the Ancient Middle East, for helping me to find and feed the roots of my religious life. And to my friends in the Abwoon Interspiritual Leadership Program, thanks for your good company and for dancing with me along the way, in such sweetness and joy.

Thanks to Max Rivers, Nancy Post, and Linda Noonan for your companionship in the land of Big Projects. And thanks to Bella Pezzati for your careful eye.

And finally, though I've thanked you in the Afterword, let me say again, thank you to Matthew van der Giessen for conversing with me so deeply through your images. And to Lynna Schaefer, thank you, thank you, thank you—for your user-friendly transliterations, yes, and most of all, for accompanying me with such joy through these gates. And, as always, thank you to Wendy, beloved partner in all.

Table of Contents

to our teacher, Shefa Gold

Introduction

Prologue: Who I Am and What This Is

In the letters and poems that follow, I write to a group of spiritual companions who share the same contemporary Jewish mystic for a teacher. I write to my friends daily as a way of engaging in the practice called "counting the *Omer*," a spiritual discipline that marks the forty-nine days between the spring festival of *Pesach* (Passover) and the early summer festival of *Shavuot*, the "Festival of Weeks," that is the Hebrew foundation for the Christian celebration of Pentecost. For the first two springs, my companions and I reflected together on the forty-nine days, with several of us acting as guides for the others, each of us taking a one week period. I fell in love with the practice immediately, and by the third year I was sending out daily messages with poems for each of the forty-nine days. Those missives, with a bit of commentary directed toward you, reader, have become this book.

I converted to Judaism in the summer of 2008. My partner Wendy and I like to call this event my "Convergence" as it seems to us not a turning away from but a joining of lineages. Before I converged, Wendy and I had lived together for thirty-three years, rearing two children well into their teen and young adult years. We sustained a bi-religious household through more than twenty of those years. There is no accounting for timing. It's beyond me.

Our way of life—Wendy attending synagogue with the child of her womb, and I going to church with the child of my womb—was the one that had integrity for us at the time. We wanted our children to have a religious foundation, and we believed that the religion given to each of us at birth should be honored, at the very least, by exploring our relationship to that religion. So that is what we did. It was a scheduling nightmare, but we managed.

What changed for me? In my early thirties, after a young adulthood of no-church, I reconnected with the tradition of my childhood by joining an urban Methodist church, politically progressive and theologically liberal. But as fine as the preaching in this church could be, and as lovely and familiar the people, something about the worship did not satisfy. I needed more silence, more depth, more sense of life in prayer than I was experiencing in the services I attended. To supplement the worship, I found a spiritual director who was an Episcopal priest, and I explored more contemplative practices with her. I rose early weekday mornings for a year to pray and receive the Eucharist with the Episcopal nuns of St. Margaret's House in Philadelphia, where we live. I explored Taize and Centering Prayer. I progressed through the Ignatian Exercises under the guidance of my director. But when I learned, through the work of scholar and poet Neil Douglas-Klotz, that Jesus would have been praying and teaching in Aramaic, close cousin to ancient Hebrew and the *lingua franca* of his day, and in Biblical Hebrew, I began to understand my restlessness in a new way. [1] Christianity is the only major religion that does not pray and study in the language of its prophet.

When I first encountered Douglas-Klotz's transliteration and poetic translations of the Lord's Prayer from Aramaic, I was stunned. My jaw, quite literally, dropped: I wanted the words in my mouth. I began to memorize the Aramaic syllables and to pray them daily. In the years that followed, I studied with Douglas-Klotz, in person and through books and audio publications. I developed a practice of praying in Aramaic for nearly ten years while engaged in the Unitarian Universalist Church that our younger son and I had joined after leaving the Methodist church. Although I brought some of the Aramaic Jesus teachings to this church as a lay worship leader, for the most part my prayer life and my church life were quite separate. Throughout those years, I attended a Reconstructionist synagogue with my partner on high holidays and other special services. As I explored the Semitic Jesus, I became more attentive to the Hebrew as well as the Aramaic in the Jewish services I attended. In truth I was envious of the regular communal engagement with the ancient languages that I experienced in the synagogue.

Yet my longing and envy did not indicate to me that I might want to become Jewish. For me, that would take a big step away from habitual ways of thinking about who I was and what I could be. In 2004, following my nose toward the ancients, I approached Rabbi Phyllis Berman, a member of my partner's synagogue whose voice, readings,

translations, and teachings from Hebrew text profoundly
moved me. I asked if she would be my spiritual director.
When she readily and radiantly agreed, I was flooded with
a delicious and mysterious joy. I followed the joy into
several years of regular spiritual conversation with Phyllis,
as I and my younger son continued to participate in the
Unitarian Universalist Church.

In conversation with Rabbi Phyllis, I was exposed to the
wisdom of her teacher, Jewish Renewal Rabbi Shefa Gold,
whose special modality is Hebrew chant. Continuing to
follow my nose, seeds of joy popping within me, I sought
out my spiritual director's teacher. I wrote to Shefa Gold
and told her that, although I wasn't Jewish, I was seeking
her on a hunch. I spoke of my hunger for the Hebrew roots
of Christianity. On the basis of my letter and the strength of
Phyllis Berman's recommendation, Shefa Gold welcomed
me into her chant leadership training. Although I had no
particular interest in leading Hebrew chanting that I was
aware of at the time, I did have a keen interest in spending
time with this teacher, and I encouraged my partner Wendy
(the more musical of the two of us and definitely the more
Jewish!) to join me, which she did. I was to be the first
non-Jew in Shefa's training program. We completed the
program known as *Kol Zimra* (Voice of Song) in the winter
of 2008. I "converged" with Judaism the following
summer. The bulk of the *Omer* letters were composed in
the spring of 2010.

More of the story of my convergence unfolds in the letters and poems that follow. Here I want to say a bit about the poems contained within the letters. Writing and speaking poetry has been my clear calling for most of my life. Perhaps the calling first came to me when I was eight, sitting beneath the amber lamp of my Great Aunt's study and reading aloud to her. Or perhaps I felt the call when I was six and, lying face-up on my porch step, heard something like my name uttered from the clouds I watched above. When I was fifteen I knew without doubt I would go through my life as poet. By that time I was reading, hearing, absorbing the voices of the poets whose words gave me strength, clarity, the sense of mystery, and the music I needed to begin becoming adult in this world. Dylan Thomas, e.e. cummings, William Carlos Williams. I memorized their lines. I began to write my own poems then and to ponder how to be a poet in the world—how *I* might do *that*.

When I was twenty-eight, a therapist with whom I was working asked me to name three things that I wanted most in life. One of the three was this: I wanted to make poems that were beautifully crafted and useful to others in their everyday lives. Counting the *Omer* is a practice of exploring and honoring daily life. I offer the poems within these letters as helpers—pitchers for pouring out the blessings of each day, bowls or cups to hold them, or keys, perhaps, to open the doors that may hide them.

The Omer, Kabbalah, and the Tree of Life

In the Jewish calendar, the *Omer* encompasses the seven weeks between the Festival of *Pesach*, or Passover, and *Shavuot*, the Festival of Weeks. The practice of counting the days of the *Omer* has its origin in the agricultural world of the Biblical Jews, when barley was the first crop of the spring harvest. An *omer* is a measure of a sheaf of barley. The Book of Leviticus instructs: "You shall bring an *omer* of the first fruits of your harvest to the priest; and he shall wave the *omer* before God to be acceptable for you" (Lev. 23:10-11).

> And from the day on which you bring the sheaf of elevation offering—the day after the Sabbath—you shall count off seven weeks. They must be complete: you must count until the day after the seventh week—fifty days; then you shall bring an offering of new grain to God (Lev. 23:15-16).

And in Deuteronomy:

> You shall count off seven weeks; start to count the seven weeks when the sickle is first put to the standing grain. Then you shall observe the Feast of Weeks for the Lord your God, offering your freewill contribution according as the Lord your God has blessed you (Deut.16:9-10)

For the ancient Jews, counting the *Omer*, waving the measure of barley, marked the beginning of the harvest season that culminated with the all-important wheat crop. It was a celebration of gratitude for what was received, the barley, and an expression of hope for what will come: the wheat. We may well imagine it was a time of anxiety also, as the prosperity of the entire year depended upon the yield from these two crops.

The linkage of *Pesach* and *Shavuot* through the counting of the weeks, a relationship not specified in scripture, was a development of priestly and rabbinic thought, with some struggle between the priests and the rabbis over the exact day that the counting should start.[2] With the destruction of the Temple and the scattering of the Jewish people in the early centuries of the Common Era, the importance of the priestly class shrank, agriculture became less important as a means of livelihood for the scattered people, and rabbinic Judaism took hold. The early spring period became associated with the liberation of the Jews from Egypt, and became the Festival of *Pesach* (Passover). And with the rising influence of the Rabbis came a new understanding of the significance of *Shavuot*. As delineated in the *Talmud*, the holy book of rabbinic writings from this period, *Shavuot* marked the receiving of *Torah*, the divine revelation given through Moses at Sinai as covenant between God and the Jewish people, newly liberated from slavery in Egypt but still wandering. The practice of counting the *Omer* now joined these two formative events for the Jewish people. The special counting delineated a period of spiritual preparation for receiving the covenant of love in the wilderness; the seven weeks became a time of self-scrutiny and soul work. As described by Rabbi Min

Kantrowitz, "The desire for a bountiful wheat crop that could feed our bodies became metaphorically transformed into a desire for spiritual connection, a longing for wisdom and enlightenment, a preparation for revelation." [3]

Kabbalah (literally, "receiving") is the Hebrew word for the Jewish mystical path, an evolving body of stories, teachings, and practices that emphasize awareness and experience of the Divine. Kabbalistic writings encourage the active development of an intimate relationship with God. Mystics of all faiths have developed many ways of understanding and exploring the channels of divine flow through human beings. One way is represented by the Kabbalistic Tree of Life, a model that describes ten aspects, ten *sephirot*, of God. The idea that there are attributes of the divine that can be "examined and searched among" can be traced as far back as the *Sefer Yetzirah* (Book of Formation), a mystical text compiled in the third to sixth centuries of the Common Era.[4] The word *sephira* (singular of *sephirot*) is related to the Hebrew root SFR, "to count" or "to number." Mystics have pointed out that the word also carries the meanings of *sipur*, telling a story, and *sapir*, a sapphire stone.[5] Over time, the ten *sephirot* evolved into the diagram known as the Tree of Life, an imaginative representation of the way Divine Essence moves and becomes manifest through physical form. For Jewish mystics the Tree of Life has become central to the practice of counting the *Omer*.

The Human Body And
The Tree Of Life

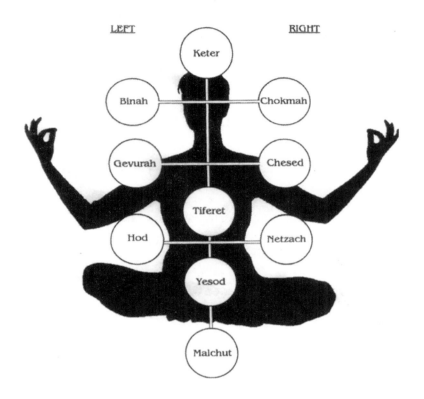

The *sephirot* relevant to counting the *Omer* are the lower seven. The upper three are known as the "upper *sephirot*." They are:

> **Keter**: Crown, point of God contact
>
> **Hochma**: Wisdom, rooted in knowledge and experience
>
> **Binah**: Understanding, ability to perceive and explain meaning

Since the upper three *sephirot* are considered closest to the divine realm, we can only glimpse their impact on our lives occasionally. The seven lower *sephirot* are the facets of the Divine that are more readily accessible to ordinary human beings in everyday life. Hence they are the attributes that provide the framework for counting the *Omer*. Qualities and symbols associated with the *sephirot* have accumulated and evolved over the centuries. These are commonly held associations for the seven lower *sephirot*:

> **Chesed**: loving-kindness, grace, benevolence
>
> **Gevurah**: strength, justice, limits, boundaries
>
> **Tiferet**: beauty, harmony, balance, compassion
>
> **Netzach**: endurance, victory, physical energy, persistence
>
> **Hod**: splendor, humility, glory of physical forms
>
> **Yesod**: intimacy, foundation, long-lasting relationship

Malchut/Shechina: leadership, sovereignty, integrity, indwelling presence of the Divine

The seven lower *sephirot* have become the major gateways, or portals, for the seven weeks of the *Omer*, with one aspect arching over each of the seven weeks. Additionally, each day of the week corresponds to one of the seven attributes. We might think of the structure of the *Omer* as a series of gates within gates. The first week we enter through the gate of loving-kindness and then, within that territory of gentle love, we encounter, on each successive day, loving-kindness again, then justice, beauty, endurance, splendor, intimacy, leadership, and so on.

Every day, with its unique correspondences, presents a dynamic tension between two attributes of the Divine that move within us. Each day is an opportunity to explore the challenges and blessings of a complex, multi-faceted, and at times arrestingly simple Divine Love. The experience of the mystics tells us that Divine Flow moves through the physical form, perpetually emanating from and returning to Source. Heavenly Energy flowing through humans is embodied energy. To help us work with the energies as they flow through our bodies, the mystics have mapped the *sephirot* on the human form.

Counting the *Omer* the mystic's way is more than a mental exercise, more than a way of thinking or talking about the self and God, or a diagram for self-improvement. We engage wholly in this process—physically, emotionally, intellectually, and spiritually. Counting the *Omer* is something we do and something we let happen to and through us. When we count as a mystic counts, we set our intention, our *kavannah*, to the possibilities of waking up to the presence of the Divine in our ordinary lives. We invite into everyday life the power and ease of an unobstructed Divine Flow. Counting the *Omer*, we prepare ourselves daily for the experience of Divine Revelation, not only in a grand way at Sinai, on *Shavuot*, the festival that closes our seven weeks of conscious counting, but every day, every seemingly ordinary moment, when the gates of our awareness are open.

How to Use this Book

These writings offer company and encouragement as you move through the practice of counting the *Omer*. The daily reflections and poems I've included are an invitation to attend to the quieter voices and subtler energies of your life, voices easy to miss in the rush-rush, flash-flash of contemporary daily life. The book is meant to be read day by day, each passage on its numbered day. For those new to the practice of counting the *Omer*, I include instructions on how to count the traditional way—beginning the second night of Passover, standing, after sundown, on the eve of each changing day. The traditional prayers, in transliterations of the Hebrew and in English, are at the head of each section. Because I believe there is power in

the sounds of the ancient tongue, the transliterations have
been specially adapted for non-Hebrew speakers to come
close to the sound of the Hebrew, at least as it is currently
spoken in synagogues. Say the prayers in either or both of
the languages, as you are comfortable. I recommend saying
the prayers in the traditional way at the traditional time—
sometime during the dark of the evening, perhaps just
before bed—and counting in the formal way. Doing so, we
set our intentions for the following day, and we affirm our
connection with generations who have counted before us.
Having said that, let it be known the first year I counted I
did none of this. I jumped in feet first—I wasn't even
officially Jewish yet. Knowing very little about the *Omer*
except the chart of daily attributes, I experienced the days
as I found them. You, too, will find your way.

On the following day, set aside time to read, or re-read, the
messages for each day. You will find that they read well
aloud. Say them to yourself or to a close companion. If
you've forgotten the traditional count of the evening
before, don't worry, just move on to the day's writings. If
you forget a few days in a row, go ahead and catch up with
the caravan. You don't have to say the traditional blessings
if you've forgotten the evening count—they are really
meant for a particular point in time. Most of us fall out of
line once in a while. So do the best you can—strive to keep
count consistently, but don't stress over mistakes. You are
always welcome back.

Each day's entry will include a letter to my *Kol Zimra* companions, within which is a poem of mine I have selected to help carry the energy of the day, as well as a message to you. Allow in your day some time for personal reflection. This may include journal or letter writing, art making, chanting or other music, yoga, sitting meditation, conversations with friends, a combination of any of these, or something else that works for you. The important thing here is to *do* something with the *Omer*, not just think, but do. As I've said, counting the *Omer* by the Tree of Life is more than a mental exercise or a topic of discussion. The *sephirot* are portals, actual gateways to a deepening and expanding awareness of an extraordinary beauty: the heaven that hovers within and all around our so-called ordinary lives. The gates open to us when we open to them.

between the doors

all things are possible
i don't mean my house or yours
i don't mean inside or out
that space between
is where i'll meet you

let's stop this back and forth
let's stay right here
in the doorway
where all wars cease

it may seem like a narrow place
where nothing much
could happen

but we can not know the size
of openings we do not see
nor feel the breadth of
that which waits for us

the other side of what seems
impossible

Through the gates we go then—let's see what awaits us.

Susan Windle

Notes

[1] Neil Douglas-Klotz, *Prayers of the Cosmos: Meditations on the Aramaic Work of Jesus* (New York: HarperCollins, 1990) 1-3.

[2] Arthur I. Waskow, *Seasons of our Joy: A Handbook of Jewish Festivals* (Toronto; New York: Bantam, 1982) 165-169.

[3] Min Kantrowitz, *Counting the Omer: A Kabbalastic Meditation Guide* (Santa Fe: Gaon, 2010) 13.

[4] Edward Hoffman, *The Way of Splendor: Jewish Mysticism and Modern Psychology, Updated 25th Anniversary ed.* (Lanham, MD: Bowman & Littlefield, 2007) 44.

[5] Simon Jacobson, *A Spiritual Guide to Counting the Omer: Forty-Nine Steps to Personal Refinement According to the Jewish Tradition* (New York, NY: Vaad Hanachos Hatmimim, 1996) 4.

The Forty-Nine Gates

Preparation for the Journey

Dear One,

Every journey begins before the beginning. Pilgrimages take a bit of preparation. We must set our intention: where do we want to go and why? What yearning sends us on our way? What gifts do we bring, and what do we hope to gain from our pilgrimage? And we must gather what's needed for the road. For this walk through the gates of the *Omer*, you do not need much. This book can be enough. If there is a musical instrument central to your soul's expression, bring that. A yoga mat might be handy. Meditation pillow, perhaps. A gift for your host, definitely—something you'd like to offer of yourself, something you value highly: your curiosity perhaps, your sense of humor, your love of beauty, compassion, or your basic willingness to engage, to participate, perhaps, in something new. You choose.

Before we enter the first gate of the *Omer*, take time to prepare. To line up your counting with the Jewish calendar, begin on the second evening of Passover. Remember that a day begins and ends at sundown, so Day 1 of the *Omer* starts in the evening and continues the following day until the sun sets. A table can help you keep track of the days in case you are concerned about losing track, as I certainly was in the first year of counting. If you don't have a Jewish calendar, you may want to number the days on your Gregorian calendar to help you.

Once your calendar is in order, or perhaps as you are preparing it, breathe gently with the question: *What do I long for that I hope to find on this journey through the forty-nine gates?* Sometimes a hand resting softly over the area around your heart can help this process. After a bit of silence and attentive breathing, when you are moved, take note of your yearning in whatever way feels comfortable for you. What you long for may show itself to you in words, in images, or both. You may choose to sing or hum a melody, move with your yearning, simply say it aloud, or draw it with your finger on the floor. Allow yourself to be surprised by what you hear and see. Whatever it is that comes to you, whether in word, image, sound, or movement, say thank you.

Now use the same process for something you would like to change about yourself or your life. This could be a habit you'd like to break, a part of yourself you want to expand, a talent that wants more expression, a fear or a worry that seems to hold you back, or something you are not doing that you wish you were doing. Think of this as your personal sacrifice for this pilgrimage, what you will offer up for transformation. Don't fuss over this part too much. Of whatever comes to you make a note, knowing this is exactly the right sacrifice for you to offer. Remember to say thank you for whatever information you receive.

And now we are nearly ready to set out. The counting begins always after sundown, always in the darkness. The first of the seven lower *sephirot* beckons us. *Chesed*, the divine attribute of loving-kindness, arches over the first week of the *Omer*. Before we begin, we will say the traditional blessing for every beginning:

bah'Ruch ah'Tah ahdoh'Nai, ehloh'Heynu Meh'lehch ha'oh'Lahm, sheheh'chee'Ahnu v'key'ih'Mahnu v'hihgee'Ahnu, lah'z'mahn ha'Zeh

> Blessed are you, our God, sovereign of the universe, who has kept us in life, sustained us, and permitted us to reach this season.

(A note about the transliterations: this is a non-traditional transliteration system. It is meant to 'read' the way Hebrew sounds. The capitalized syllable is where the major stress lies. The letters '*ch*' are guttural, somewhat stronger than the sound at the end of Bach.)

And now let's say the traditional meditation for preparing to count the *Omer*:

> Behold I am ready and prepared to fulfill the *mitzvah* of counting the *Omer*, as it says in the *Torah*: "You shall count from the eve of the second day of *Pesach*, when an *omer* of grain is to be brought as an offering, seven complete weeks. The day after the seventh week of your counting will make fifty days. (Leviticus 23:15-16)

Week One: *Chesed*
Loving-kindness, grace, benevolence

Day 1
Chesed sh'b'Chesed: **Love within Love**

(Eve of the first day of the *Omer*.)

*bah'Ruch ah'Tah ahdoh'Nai, ehloh'Heynu Meh'lehch
ha'oh'Lahm, ah'Shair k'd'Shahnu b'meetz'vo'Tahv,
v'tzee'Vahnu Ahl s'fee'Raht hah'O'mer*

> Blessed are You, God, Source of Loving-kindness,
> You make us holy through Your *mitzvot*,
> commanding us to count the *Omer*.

ha'Yoam Yoam eh'Chod l'O'mer

> Today is the first day of the *Omer*.

Okay, Dear One, here we go. The daily letters to my
spiritual companions begin below. I am inviting you to
enter, witness, engage. I will address you, as I have
already begun to do, as "Dear One" and the *Kol Zimra*
companions as "Beloved Wanderers," or "Beloveds"
to help you recognize which kind of message you are
reading. Please know we are all beloveds, all
wanderers, all dear.

Beloved Wanderers,

Welcome to the entrance of the forty-nine gates. We begin
the counting by passing through the gate of loving-
kindness—that fundamental benevolence at the source of
our being. Love is the fundamental energy of this week and

the special lens through which we view our lives. To enter
the gate of this particular day, the gate of mercy within
mercy, is to receive a double portion of love, extra fuel for
the journey, a journey that can be excruciatingly
complicated and one that must be held always within a
framework of kindness; kindness toward self and kindness
toward others. Receiving the blessings of this day can be
like falling into the face of a flower, a soft landing that
changes you thoroughly. Whatever else you may have
thought you were about, this is the flower you have been
seeking. Eat, drink now. You are thoroughly at home in this
fragrance, familiar and delicious— the very walls welcome
you. This is what you were meant for, sweet bee. This is
how you do your love-work, work built on the shoulders of
many before you, and meant to nourish generations after
you. By simply receiving what is here in these petals, you
accomplish the goals of this gate. Can you allow yourself to
be completely and thoroughly accepted? Can you let
yourself be who, what, and how you are, extending as you
do that same acceptance outward? This is how you grow
and how you help others grow. Enter this gate and receive
the abundance of unconditional love that is available to
you, right here, right now. You will take this gift with you
as you pass through every other gate on your journey.

Heavenly Blue

This is the blue that sees you.

Its clear gaze asks nothing,

wants nothing, misses nothing.

All is forgiven in this flower.

What you cannot accept,
what you outright reject

is taken up in these petals
and turned, held, fed and clothed,

returned to you in a yellow robe

to move like a god
through this world.

All blessings on your travels.

Susan/Shoshana Asiel

Well, Dear One, can you allow yourself to be completely and thoroughly accepted? Can you let yourself be who, what, and how you are; extending as you do that same acceptance outward? Can you let others be who they are? Can you let reality be what it is? Practice that, all day long. Be especially kind to the part of you that judges and rejects.

A word about my name. You have seen that I sign off as "Susan/Shoshana Asiel." The first is the name my parents gave me, the second, my Hebrew name; I took it when I became Jewish. It means "Lily, made of

God." Or "God-made Lily." I am growing into it. I use both names to affirm both realities. It's a practice.

Day 2
Gevurah sh'b'Chesed: **Strength within Love**

(Eve of the second day of the *Omer*.)

bah'Ruch ah'Tah ahdoh'Nai, ehloh'Heynu Meh'lehch ha'oh'Lahm, ah'Shair k'd'Shahnu b'meetz'vo'Tahv, v'tzee'Vahnu Ahl s'fee'Raht hah'O'mer.

> Blessed are You, God, Source of Loving-kindness,
> You make us holy through Your *mitzvot*,
> commanding us to count the *Omer*.

ha'Yoam Yoam Shnay yo'Meem l'O'mer.

> Today is the second day of the *Omer*.

Dear One, how was your first day? Take note. Say thank you for everything received.

Beloved Wanderers,

Welcome to the second day, the gate of strength within the gate of love and acceptance. This morning, the dawning of a day that was to be filled with the very essence of loving-kindness (so I told myself), a day that should have rested in the gentleness at the heart of things, I awoke with a heaviness about my head and a familiar tightness in the chest. Perhaps an excess of Passover wine accounted for the headache. The constriction in my heart and breath was something else again: a distinctly unkind feeling that arrives mysteriously in the night sometimes and greets me with a restive grunt upon my waking. The antithesis of *Chesed*-ness, this mood carries an anxiety about self and the world, self in the world: how will I perform, or how have I performed, the challenges set before me? In this mood, the report card of my life is appallingly mediocre and my expectations of the future dim. What did I think I was doing offering to post these writings every day for forty- nine days? Where exactly was I going to find the time to do that? These were my waking thoughts on the first day of the *Omer*. How disappointing.

Anticipating the evening's post, I looked up my notes for the second day in last year's counting. I found this poem:

Prodigal Daughter

When all else failed you came home
with nothing to show for your time
no PhD no published book
nothing in your hands at all
nothing on your back
nothing up your sleeve
nothing to show but your face
broken and beautiful (some whispered)
cracked with light.

She gave a banquet in your honor.
You tried to say, *It was just, just that—*

but she wouldn't let you explain
Your face! Your face! she said
and treated you as if you were holy.

Which is how you have felt about her.

Nothing in your life is what you expect.
You scoured the world for praise
and find yourself celebrated here
for nothing at all but your face.

Why this poem for the second day? My first inclination, in
that heart-clenching frame of mind, was to dismiss
whatever I had in mind last year. It was after all a poem
with reference to Christian scripture and this is a Jewish
practice. If the poem were to be useful at all surely it
should have been the first poem. Why did I begin with that
blue flower anyway? So my mind ran on… But since I
have chosen to consciously engage in this spiritual practice,
I reined in my thoughts and chose to follow the trail I left
last year, trusting the intuition that picked the poem in the
first place. It was the kinder thing to do—kinder to
myself—so the day's gate whispered to me, and because I
am counting gates, I listened.

Over breakfast I made a few notes about this evening's post
and the Prodigal poem, and then went about my business.
As the day wore on, though, my headache worsened; my
gut began to churn, so that by mid-afternoon, with a half
hour between meetings and a blessedly available couch, I
was supine. Breathing gently into and around my heart

area, I remembered the heavenly flower, how it would feel to fall into the petals… Next I knew, I was awaking from a nap of divine proportions. Head clear. Heart doors open. Ready for the rest of the day.

Now it is evening, and I want to tell you something about the second day of the *Omer*. In that "Prodigal Daughter" poem, a piece I wrote for my mother when I was a thirty-six, I usually identify with the daughter, the wandering one, perennially returning. Today though, it is the mother who draws me, the perpetually gracious host. I am calling home the scattered pieces of myself. I am the woman standing tall in the doorway with open arms. There will be a great celebration when the children come home. To give a party, a really good party, takes a certain kind of strength, doesn't it? We must pull ourselves together in order to open properly and receive our guests. Discipline, *Gevurah*, beloveds, is at the core of love. May you find within you the strength you need for the work ahead.

Have a blessed day. Listen to the gates.

All love,

Susan/Shoshana Asiel

On this day, Dear One, you may want to pay special attention to the parts of you that collapse, give in to worry and anxiety, or distract you in any way from what's most important to you. Or you may not want to, but you may decide to pay attention anyway, since, after all, it is *Gevurah* day, and *Chesed*, unconditional love, is the underlying reality of this and every week. Gently, warmly then, if you are willing (hand over heart and soft breath to the belly can help here), invite some parts of yourself that you would not normally choose to invite into your heart-space. Invite them, perhaps, to share a meal with you. To those parts willing to show up fully today, listen with care and appreciate the gifts they've brought you. With respect to the shy or more reluctant guests, allow them to take their time. Their presence itself is a gift to you—even if they don't make it to the table. In can be difficult to enjoy your own party, but do your best. Appreciate the great variety your soul includes. And say thank you to all for being part of your life.

Day 3
Tiferet sh'b'Chesed: Compassion within Love

(Eve of the third day of the *Omer*.)

bah'Ruch ah'Tah ahdoh'Nai, ehloh'Heynu Meh'lehch ha'oh'Lahm, ah'Shair k'd'Shahnu b'meetz'vo'Tahv, v'tzee'Vahnu Ahl s'fee'Raht hah'O'mer.

> Blessed are You, God, Source of Loving-kindness,
> You make us holy through Your *mitzvot*,
> commanding us to count the *Omer*.

ha'Yoam Yoam shlee'Shah yo'meem l'O'mer.

> Today is the third day of the *Omer*.

Dear One, I trust your second day was all that you needed it to be. I hope you are feeling deeply appreciated. If not, take a moment for that, breathing a simple "thank you" into your heart. It is always a good time for gratitude.

Beloved Wanderers,

The gate of the wide-open heart within the gate of loving-kindness. This gate challenges me to a greater openness than I feel ready for today. I look at my notes on *Tiferet sh'b' Chesed* from last year's counting, April, 2009:

> I wake up this morning on *Tiferet* day, the day of Compassion, Beauty, and Harmony within the gate of Loving-kindness, and come across a harsh place in my inner landscape. I am reading the newspaper—an article about Nicholas Hughes, the 40-year-old son of well-known poets Sylvia Plath and Ted Hughes. Nicholas, one of two toddlers left behind after the suicide of his mother, killed himself last week in his home in Fairbanks, Alaska. I feel such sorrow for this man. I weep for the legacy of abandonment left him from his mother's suicide, for the legacy of depression itself. But as I read, I notice that I feel no sorrow whatsoever for his mother, the poet whose works I admired as a young woman, but whose suicide, especially after I became a mother myself, appalled me. I feel only horror toward a mother who would carefully secure her children in a sealed room and then gas herself. Then I read on that some very short time after Sylvia killed herself, her husband, Ted Hughes, re-married. His new wife, stepmother to Sylvia's

children Nicholas and Frieda, gassed herself and her
six-month-old baby while Sylvia and Ted's children
were still young. I suppose I once knew this story
but had forgotten it. I am good at forgetting what
horrifies me. Well, since it is *Tiferet* day, I must be
especially aware of the places where compassion
doesn't flow, where pure judgment reigns, crowding
out sorrow with a sense of moral superiority.
Hughes and both of his wives are the object of my
deepest scorn. But since it is *Chesed* week, I hold
myself and my judgments in loving attention: I
notice, and I refrain from heaping more judgment
on myself.

This year I am thinking, and maybe even feeling a little,
that people who abandon their children by suicide, even
people who murder their children, are part of the ultimate
reality we call God. *k'doh'Sheem t'hee'You key kah'Doash
ah'Nee*, "You are holy, for I am holy" (Lev. 19:2), means
every "you" of the Universe, not just those of us who
behave well. The gate of *Tiferet sh'b' Chesed* invites the
heart to expand and take in that truth; the gate supports, and
encourages us to do so. It's the hardest kind of work, and
mostly I am not very good at it. But I have a sense that
opening the *Tiferet* door wider, if only by slight increments,
would be a good and healthy thing for my soul.

Here is a poem I wrote about my younger sister, whose
mental illness, diagnosed as severe paranoid schizophrenia,
is one of the faces of God that I have not wanted to let in.

Confession

I have not wanted to be
the sister I am,
sister of the once quick child,
sister of a disordered mind
endless cigarettes and repetitive
cups of tea from the flowered
china cups our mother
once loved.

When I visit the sister I am
I never want to stay.
In the stuffed apartment
smoke crowds my throat.
Pillows of every size piled high
on couch and chair
leave no room
for sitting down,
and mostly
there is nothing to say.

And there is only the same thing
to be heard, over and over,
on any given day.
Today the one thing
is about the white doves
in their cages
how they coo
to the one who cares for them
when the one who cares
is relaxed at home
with her tea.

Today I choose
the chair that leans back perpetually
in the far corner of her dim room.
The drapes here are always closed.
What lamps there are
she keeps
permanently low.
There is no difference
between night and day here
and that
is the terrible hole
I fear.

Helped by this counting, I learn not to fear quite so much. I practice falling into the holes I've tried to avoid. Something seems to catch me, and urge me on—into the deeper places.

With gratitude for this practice and for you, holy ones, who move along with me through these gates, I wish you harmony, balance, and a strong, resonant love.

Enjoy your day.

Susan/Shoshana Asiel

Well, Dear One, are there holes you've tried to avoid? Are there parts of yourself or your reality that you do not want to look at, let alone invite to share a meal with you? Be kind to yourself here; remember you are always held within the gate of kindness. Make note of everything that comes into your awareness without judgment or blame. Be a compassionate observer of your life.

Day 4
Netzach sh'b'Chesed: **Persistence in Loving**

(Eve of the fourth day of the *Omer*.)

bah'Ruch ah'Tah ahdoh'Nai, ehloh'Heynu Meh'lehch ha'oh'Lahm, ah'Shair k'd'Shahnu b'meetz'vo'Tahv, v'tzee'Vahnu Ahl s'fee'Raht hah'O'mer.

> Blessed are You, God, Source of Loving-kindness, You make us holy through Your *mitzvot*, commanding us to count the *Omer*.

ha'Yoam Yoam arbah'Ah yo'meem l'O'mer.

> Today is the fourth day of the *Omer*.

How are you doing, Dear One, with your compassionate witnessing? You may want to spend a little time in meditation here: breathing into your heart as you review, in your mind's eye, your third day—the ups and downs, challenges and blessings. Remember to say thank you for everything you see and for all you've experienced so far on these the beginning days of your journey.

Beloveds,

Today we open to the benevolence of *Netzach*, the
goodness that comes of keeping a steady pace toward a
clear goal. Year by year, I inch closer to full-hearted
acceptance of my sister's life as it is, as she is. My sister's
name is Meg, though I usually speak of her as "my sister." I
cannot connect the woman she has become with the child I
knew. For the first ten years of her diagnosis, I simply
denied the presence of schizophrenia, the illness that
overtook her as a young married woman. That couldn't be
right, not my little sister, the bright, funny, and determined
little girl I had known growing up. She had a very nice
husband and an adorable child—all would be well with a
bit of psychotherapy. When I finally had to accept the
diagnosis—the evidence was all too clear—I became adept
at distracting myself from its painful reality; I would
simply forget about Meg for long swaths of time, waking
up only when some emergency, usually involving the
police and forced hospitalizations, erupted into my daily
life. Then, in a state of barely suppressed panic, I would run
over from Philadelphia to the coast of South Jersey where
she lives and "deal with" the situation as best I could.
When the crisis was over, I would forget again. Once, in a
really big crisis after her marriage broke up, I agreed to
have Meg live with us. I thought that perhaps if I had her
with me all the time I could be more effective at controlling
the chaos. That didn't work.

Eventually, worn out by the pattern of denial and sudden reactivity, I began the long march toward acceptance of things as they are. I started living with the question, "How might I be genuinely helpful to my sister without hurting self or family?" I have come to cultivate, however painstakingly, a quiet, attentive resignation to what is true, *and* I make regular visits not tied to crises.

Netzach, today's gate, is the quality of endurance, the ability to envision a goal and proceed towards it. With long vision and a steady pace, I am spared the roller coaster of denial and rude awakening. I look toward the kind of love I want to give. I hold a commitment to visit Meg monthly, whether I feel like it or not, and I become a part of the rhythm of her life, allowing her to become part of the rhythm of mine. I do not do this perfectly. There are months I miss from busy-ness or neglect. But when kindness and compassion are absent on the emotional level, the quality of *Netzach* can carry me on, moving me slowly toward the love I want to embody, however far away I may feel from the experience of that love.

Sometimes I get a glimpse of something shimmering closer than I think.

Zeh Dodi

This is my beloved, my friend.
(Song of Songs 5:16)

My little sister, forty-seven now,
turns from the lock in her door and
steps toward my car. There's a sliver of light
around her pale head and denim dress.
Someone, tracing her with a golden thread,
relaxes my hands on the steering wheel.
Whose eyes are these
I look through now? Sunlight
drapes around my shoulders:
yellow silk.

My sister slides into the passenger's seat,
hauling the enormous brown
bag that swallows her keys.
I do not know what to say
after "How are you?
"Did you get to your program?
Have you done your shopping,
taken your meds?"

On the way to her lap, my sister's eyes,
Atlantic blue, linger in my gaze
long enough to pour
the family ocean into the cup
I didn't know I held.
My sister's hair, returned from red rinse to
girlhood blonde, though ashy now, is fine
as the Jersey sand I kiss.

I am grateful
to tumble together
in the same salt.
I want to love always
like this.

Beyond all that perplexes and disturbs, something glows, beckons, assures. Because of that glimmer, I travel on— with faith in the kindness that holds us all.

Enjoy the day, beloveds. Enjoy the day.

Towards love,

with love,

Susan/Shoshana Asiel

Dear One, perhaps there is something you think you cannot do but want to do? Or something you think you must do but resist doing? Something that feels entirely too large, a goal out of reach, perhaps? An unfulfilled longing? If something comes to mind now or in the course of your day, hold your desire and your obstacles lovingly within the gate of *Netzach sh'b'Chesed*, Persistence within Loving. Trust that you will find your way.

Day 5
Hod sh'b'Chesed: **The Humble Glory of Loving**

(Eve of the fifth day of the *Omer*.)

bah'Ruch ah'Tah ahdoh'Nai, ehloh'Heynu Meh'lehch
ha'oh'Lahm, ah'Shair k'd'Shahnu b'meetz'vo'Tahv,
v'tzee'Vahnu Ahl s'fee'Raht hah'O'mer.

> Blessed are You, God, Source of Loving-kindness,
> You make us holy through Your *mitzvot*,
> commanding us to count the *Omer*.

ha'Yoam Yoam chamee'Shah yo'meem l'O'mer.

> Today is the fifth day of the *Omer*.

Good evening again, Dear One. Blessings on your fifth
day!

Beloveds,

Nothing to do in this gate but surrender—yield to the glory
of the ground. During this time of the year, in Northwest
Philadelphia where I live, the ground truly does sing its
glory. A quiet hum rises from lawns and the nearby forest
floor to fill the first green breaths of the hardwoods.
Everywhere daffodils trumpet, and all month long too,
ecstatic, glad-to-be-back forsythia goes on and on with its
wild, ungainly reach. Relax and stretch into love, whispers
the gate of *Hod* in *Chesed*. Come into your glory like these
bright flowers. This is your time, enjoy it.

April Poem

Washed in April
veiled in grey
the star magnolia opens.
In her fingers
I am lifted
to the tips of budding maples
and brushed
an early green
in the morning rain.

There you will find me still
wet, with daffodils.

I think with this poem, written seventeen years ago, I have composed my epitaph. Though I had never heard of the *Omer*, I encountered the gate of *Hod* on a walk in my neighborhood. With its soft '*h*' and closing '*d*', *Hod* is both a breath and a seal—a seal that is at once a closing, and a doorway, an opening. The ancient word, with three simple sounds, celebrates the cycles of birth and death and birth again with the '*o*' of wonder that lies between. *Hod sh' b'Chesed* asks us to love like this: with our deaths continually before us and the wonder of our lives emanating from every pore. Relax and let yourself spread into the glory that you are. Practice loving from the ground up.

I don't fret about my sister, or any other disturbance in the universe, when I give in to the wonder of *Hod*. I accept what is and praise it—grow from there.

All love always,

Susan/Shoshana Asiel

Ah, Dear One, may you, too, be lifted by the glory beneath your feet, on this and every day. Take some time outdoors today, if only five or ten minutes, to walk with awareness of the ground, whatever ground you happen to be treading, whether pavement, lawn, or forest floor. Step with awareness of the way your feet meet the surface that supports you. Do not try to change anything about this. Simply notice and accept the relationship continually available to you from the earth through the soles of your feet. As you walk, notice what you see, hear, feel… Say thank you for every experience.

Day 6
Yesod sh'b'Chesed: Commitment with Love

(Eve of the 6th day of the *Omer*)

bah'Ruch ah'Tah ahdoh'Nai, ehloh'Heynu Meh'lehch ha'oh'Lahm, ah'Shair k'd'Shahnu b'meetz'vo'Tahv, v'tzee'Vahnu Ahl s'fee'Raht hah'O'mer.

Blessed are You, God, Source of Loving-kindness,
You make us holy through Your *mitzvot*,
commanding us to count the *Omer*.

ha'Yoam Yoam shee'Shah yo'meem l'O'mer.

Today is the sixth day of the *Omer*.

Hello again. I hope you enjoyed the earth today, your splendid home. If you forgot or in any way neglected your most intimate surroundings, take heart! This is a new day with a new gate to guide you. May the ever-loving strength of *Yesod* enter your dreams tonight…

Beloveds,

Commitment within Love. There is a pleasurable tingling throughout my left hand and arm today. I've felt this before. I noticed it first in the winter of 2008 when I decided to be Jewish. The decision, as right as it felt, startled me at the time. I had lived with my Jewish partner for over 30 years without feeling inclined to convert. I had spent my entire life confirmed in the notion that I was not and would never, could never, be Jewish. So much for what I think I know. That winter, shortly after I announced my intention to Wendy and to our teacher Shefa, I began spontaneously chanting the words from *Hosea* that accompany the traditional practice of winding in *T'fillin*, preparation for morning prayers. This is a chant Shefa taught us in one of our training weeks. I had never fully learned the melody or the words in the training, but now, in the dark of morning, vowels tumbled out of my mouth, consonants a little fuzzy—I looked the words up later—the melody was not quite right but close enough.[6] And with the chanting, I noticed a pleasant tingling in my left arm, where the leather strap of the *T'fillin* would be. I was wound in a prayer I did not yet know:

v'Erestich-li L'Olam. v'Erestich-li b'Tzedek, u v'Mishpat, u'v'Chesed, u'v'Rachamim. v'Erestich-li b'EmuNah, v'yaDaat et Yah.

> I betroth you to me forever; I betroth you to me
> with Justice, with Impeccability, with Kindness, and
> Compassion. I betroth you to me with Faithfulness,
> so that you shall know God, the Breath of Life.
> (Hos. 2:21-2)

I learned the Hebrew words, and began to chant them daily. Sometimes I experienced the words and melody coming towards me, as if they were being sung to me even as I sang them out. I wrote this poem:

Betrothal (v'Erestich-li L'Olam)

> Even though I don't have the words for it
> even though I caught only a shred of the
>   phrase,
>
> thread of meaning, whisper of melody,
> I sing it back to you, as you gave it,
>
> hum the vowels in the cave of my throat.

Even though I don't have the notes right,

you tell me you are satisfied.
You say you are well-pleased.

(I saw this in the face of someone you sent
to listen.) What now do I do

with your pleasure? How live with the
        constancy
of your murmurings, the unmistakably
        flowing

delight underneath everything I am?
What more may I add to this song?

I converted to Judaism, with Shefa's help, in the waters of
the Delaware Bay in the summer of 2008. Though the
ceremony had all the ritual trappings of conversion, we
think of it more as a "convergence," a joining of lineages,
an expansion of identity, rather than a turning away from
what I was. Later that year, in the early fall, during the
month of *Elul* that followed the ceremony, I began to feel
the invisible leather wound around my left arm again. I
wrote about my post-convergence experience in my
journal:

I am now most deliciously if invisibly tethered—
softly and securely wound, whether or not I am
consciously chanting or praying. The palm of my
left hand, if I but slightly attend, is continually
receiving the flow of a prayer, which is on-going,

always there. My right arm wants to stay close, not
fly off on its own missions, but rather wait for
instructions from the left, and work together to
accomplish what needs to be done. There's a kind
of quiet ecstasy flowing through the left arm and
infusing my being, so that simply walking about on
the earth is deeply pleasurable. The rocking of my
hips as I amble—so good—and so gracious the old
trees of my neighborhood. Lovely too the beings I
encounter everywhere I go.

Now, in April, *Omer* time, I am once again delightfully
aware of my tethering. With the help of these gates I move
through my weeks with grace. Today, through the gate of
Yesod in *Chesed*, the gate of long-term love, I renew the
vows of my betrothal. I am grateful for the knowledge of
what, who, binds me in this most delicious way. The very
act of counting the *Omer*, taking measure of the day,
joining the dance of each day's particular energy, is an act
of sublime intimacy, an engagement with divine
commitment. I am so glad, delighted really, to participate in
this enduring love.

And I am grateful to be sharing it with you.

Much love,
Susan/Shoshana Asiel

And I am grateful also to you, Dear One, for beginning
to take in this story. I wonder how it works on you. I
wonder what is stirring… In the Jewish calendar, the
month of *Elul* that I referred to above is the month of

preparation that precedes *Rosh Hashanah* and *Yom Kippur*, the holidays that celebrate the creation and repentance. The Hebrew word *Elul* is an acronym for a verse from the sacred text *Shir HaShirim* (Song of Songs): *Ani l'Dodi v'Dodi Li*, which can be translated "I am my beloved's and my beloved is mine," or perhaps more accurately, "I am (toward) my beloved and my beloved is (toward) me" (Song 2:16).

Here are some questions, then, for your reflection. Take a little time with one or two of these, if you are willing. *Who is your beloved? Who or what is most dear to you? What do you most deeply value? Where is your treasure?* If you can, turn and face the face of love that comes to meet you now, this day. Spend some time considering your commitment to what matters most to you. Make a promise to yourself.

Day 7
Malchut sh'b'Chesed: The Power and Majesty of Love

(Eve of the 7th day of the *Omer*)

bah'Ruch ah'Tah ahdoh'Nai, ehloh'Heynu Meh'lehch ha'oh'Lahm, ah'Shair k'd'Shahnu b'meetz'vo'Tahv, v'tzee'Vahnu Ahl s'fee'Raht hah'O'mer.

> Blessed are You, God, Source of Loving-kindness, You make us holy through Your *mitzvot*, commanding us to count the *Omer*.

ha'Yoam Yoam sh'vee'Ee yo'meem l'O'mer.

Today is the seventh day of the *Omer*.

Greetings. I hope you are feeling well loved and divinely capable as we come to the culmination of our first week. *Mazel Tov*! We are entering the seventh day, a day of Majesty and sublime accomplishment.

Beloveds,

These are the notes I found from last year's day, written on the morning of *Malchut sh'b'Chesed*, 2009:

> I dreamed last night of Washington, DC. I was taking a job as assistant to an under-secretary of the Department of Energy or Education or Health—the job description was a little unclear, but the work was terrifically important. I would be required to live in the Capitol during the week and commute back to Philadelphia on weekends. It seemed I should take this job—after all I wanted to encourage a progressive agenda in my country—but I wondered if I'd be able to handle the details—being someone's administrative assistant does not speak to my particular strengths—and the logistics were terribly confusing: I couldn't seem to manage the labyrinth of railway tunnels between Northwest Philadelphia and DC—too many spiral staircases leading nowhere. It was a hopeless and hapless sort of dream, and I was relieved to wake from it, to find myself at home and already inhabiting my seat of power. Whew! Can it be that I do not actually have to travel an obfuscated route to do work that I am not particularly good at in order to be an effective

agent of change? Perhaps what I can do arises from the ground beneath my feet, from the roots, the depths of where I already am. That is *Malchut*, the root of true power and agency. *Malchut* in *Chesed*, power with love, majesty with kindness, is the kind of power I claim. And I don't have to go anywhere to find it—I have only to wind down into where I am, where I have been all along.

Ode to Yes

Yes.
Yes is a vulnerable word.
It leaves you wide open
like a tree.

Make the sound.
Notice the longing in the back of your
       throat.
Send it out now through your lips:
the best dream you have—
full of hope.

It doesn't matter that your leaves
will leave.
It doesn't matter what the others
see or say.
The beautiful yes of trees
will stand

and breathe
life, health
to the struggling creatures
of this world.

"So this is where the first week of counting the *Omer* lands us," I wrote in 2009, "firmly in the ground, with a wide open 'Yes' to the Tree of Life. It is a healthy place, a strong place from which to grow and change and offer sustenance."

Tonight, in 2010, I stand at the threshold of *Malchut sh' b'Chesed*, preparing to close out the week with the Majesty of Kindness. I wonder what my dreams will bring me tonight… I welcome any disturbance that may come as an agent of wisdom. For the past two nights I have dreamed of masculine power gone awry. A close friend was being physically abused by her husband, and I was trying to save her. In another dream my father, who died three years ago, showed up in a guise he often wore in life: needy and demanding emotional attention. *Yesod*, the gate that represents the active force of commitment, is associated with male genitalia. *Malchut* is associated with the female genitals, and with *Shechina*, the divine feminine. The mystics tell us that when heaven comes to earth, the divine flow will be channeled through the funnel of *Yesod* to meet and unite in joy with *Shechina* (*Malchut*). When love and power entwine all is Eden once again. May it be so—now and in the world that is coming. May I bring the two together in my life.

And you, in yours…

With love,
Susan/Shoshana Asiel

And you in yours, Dear One, and you in yours. Spend some time with a tree today. Or be a tree yourself—if yoga is your practice, do a tree pose. Do a tree pose outdoors, near a tree if you can. Notice the exquisite balance of a healthy tree—roots that drink deep and strong trunk with an upward and outward thrust. Notice how necessary it is for the limbs of trees to spread and tenderly open to receive the light through their leaves. This is how a tree lives. Consider your own life now. Are there any aspects of tree nature that could help you now—your connection to the earth perhaps, your upward and outward energy, or your ability to open and receive the nourishment you need? Ask a tree to help you find your balance, and grow.

Week Two: *Gevurah*
Strength, justice, limits, boundaries

Day 8
Chesed sh'b'Gevurah: **Love with Strength**

(Eve of the 8th day, the first day of the second week of the *Omer*.)

bah'Ruch ah'Tah ahdoh'Nai, ehloh'Heynu Meh'lehch ha'oh'Lahm, ah'Shair k'd'Shahnu b'meetz'vo'Tahv, v'tzee'Vahnu Ahl s'fee'Raht hah'O'mer

> Blessed are You, God, Source of Strength and Power, You make us holy through Your *mitzvot*, commanding us to count the *Omer*.

ha'Yoam sh'Moanah yo'Meem, sh'Heym sha'Vooah eh'Chod v'Yoam eh'Chod lah'O'mer

> Today is the eighth day of the *Omer*, which makes one week and one day of the *Omer*.

Okay, second week beginning now, Dear One. Take a moment to enjoy the moment, where you are, as you are, right here. Take a few gentle breaths in gratitude for the continuing fact of your life, the on-going presence of your being. It's all a gift. You didn't ask for it. As you would when receiving any gift, say thank you.

Beloveds,

Welcome to the second week of the *Omer*. We enter the
gate of *Gevurah* and receive gifts of strength: the ability to
set limits and practice discipline, restraint, and respect. We
will carry these gifts with us in good measure all week.
Gevurah is also associated with the quality of awe. As on
the first day of counting, we come around again to the
quality of *Chesed*, loving-kindness. Here is a note I made
last year on the day of *Chesed sh'b'Gevurah*:

> My strong, guardian love wants to keep my family,
> my children and all I care for alive and safe from
> harm today. This is the poem I choose for today:

When You First Met the Sea

for Gregory

You were three years old.
You set your buckets on the sand
and strode off on sturdy legs.
She was everything you wanted –
long white hair
and powerful arms.
Mama said
her name is *Ocean*
but you knew that she was
the most beautiful drummer
you had ever seen –
you rushed
to the shimmering
hem of her skirt.

But when you got there
her breath was wind
her beat thunder –
her wild wet dress
took your feet away!
Fear
rippled through you
like a snake
and you turned back
to the mother you knew
who was already near you
she was solid like a tree
you climbed up into her.

There is much to be afraid of in this world, so much
from which to protect ourselves and our loved ones.
Loving with *Gevurah* turns fear into awe. It's like
having the hand of God on you, this gate. I imagine
the prophets felt it. And Jacob certainly.

And now, in 2010, I am thinking again of my children. The
story of our younger son Gregory at the beach is a sweet
story. Now Wendy and I bear the challenges of launching
two sons into adulthood. In the fall, I struggled with anxiety
over our twenty-three-year-old, Gabriel, Gregory's older
brother. One year after graduating with acclaim as an
English major from the University of Pennsylvania,
Gabriel, unemployed and without direction, moved back in
with us last summer. By night, he paced our floors and
drank too much. By day, when he wasn't glued to his
laptop, pouring over Craig's List and sending out resumes,
he devoured *The Art of French Cooking* and experimented

with béarnaise and hollandaise sauces. He gained an alarming amount of weight, while our food bills swelled and my fears for him gathered, overwhelming me frequently in the darkest hours. The fear of losing a child is primal, and huge.

One night, to calm my anxiety, I searched for a way to pray for him. Seeing him again as a brilliant, strong-willed, red-haired boy, and as an intensely curious and wonder-filled toddler, I remembered the meaning of his two names, Gabriel Nathan, "God's strength," and "gift." I prayed for him that way, holding him in love and breathing the syllables of his Hebrew name: *Gavriel Natan*. I was able to go to sleep then, with the Hebrew words and the sense of his *neshema*, his soul, in my breathing.

In the daylight, I decided that Wendy and I must call him to account for how he was spending his time in our house; we must insist that he make a plan and report to us every week. And so we did, and so he agreed. Within days, he began to leave the house regularly every day for the streets of Center City Philadelphia to seek training in the culinary arts. Within two weeks he found a chef that was willing to train him, and, within another month, a paying job. He is now a line cook at a highly acclaimed Israeli restaurant in Philadelphia, happily working his way up the line in the kitchen, mentored by one of the finest young chefs in the city. If I had prayed his name in English only, would he have landed in a different restaurant? How curious the power of these ancient words…

At any rate, remembering to love our son with a prayer that connected me to his soul pulled me through a state of anxiety and helped us to set limits we needed to set. This is *Chesed sh'b'Gevurah* in action: love with strength, love with discipline.

May we pull ourselves together with love, for love. May we love ourselves pulling ourselves together—through every challenge that comes our way.

Love well, beloveds, with all your strength.

Susan/Shoshana Asiel

Well, Dear One, I wonder where this story takes you. What are your love challenges? Take a look. Notice where strength and discipline are needed in your loving. The loving you focus on today may be love of intimates in your life, your friends or family. Or it may be love of neighbor in the broad sense, the challenges of loving an enemy, or loving a particularly difficult person, or a stranger. Or perhaps love of self is what challenges you now, or love of God, whatever name or nameless sound you use for the Mystery of Creation. You may notice where and how the fear of love, or fear in love, grabs you. There is some place in your body that clenches perhaps, sometimes? If that fear-place presents itself today, you need do nothing but gently breathe there, into and around, the place of constriction. Maybe there is as an opening here, an invitation into a place wider and more wondrous…

Day 9
Gevurah sh'b'Gevurah: **Strength with Discipline**

(Eve of the 9th day, the second day of the second week of the *Omer*.)

bah'Ruch ah'Tah ahdoh'Nai, ehloh'Heynu Meh'lehch ha'oh'Lahm, ah'Shair k'd'Shahnu b'meetz'vo'Tahv, v'tzee'Vahnu Ahl s'fee'Raht hah'O'mer

> Blessed are You, God, Source of Strength and Power, You make us holy through Your *mitzvot*, commanding us to count the *Omer*.

ha'Yoam tee'Shah yo'Meem, sh'Heym sha'Vooah eh'Chod oo'Shnay yah'Meem lah'O'mer

> Today is the ninth day of the *Omer*, which makes one week and two days of the *Omer*.

Hello, Dear One. How was your eighth day? Thank you for continuing to show up, day after day… Or if you are just now returning, welcome back.

Beloveds,

Today we encounter the essence of our strength: *Gevurah sh'b'Gevurah*. We receive, in double measure today, the gifts of restraint, the ability to pull in around our core and strengthen our soul-muscles. Today we practice awe and wonder, even though we think we are too busy for this, especially because we think we are too busy. We must practice awe regularly in order to gather the energy we need for the work of living. Otherwise we will tire too soon. There is a lean intelligence to this gate. I am giving in to it.

This Day

this doorway
the one I've been ignoring
calls to me
with a deep, corpuscular
knowledge of the heart.
With clear intention—
to look, to listen only
and to record—
I step
not into hall or pathway
but onto
the muddy bottom rung
of a tall ladder
that leads
I cannot say to what.
The boughs
of the arbor above
are densest green
and what I sense are
letters
woven in the shade

illuminated nests
baskets, hanging
pouches, plump
with berries and wings
cradles in the canopy
I recognize only
by their songs
and by the way my body wants
to rise
and climb in.

The kernel at the core of *Gevurah* is the germ of our ability to give—like good yoginis, we pull in so that we may grow long in love. Like the discipline of keeping *Shabbat*, the wisdom of *Gevurah sh'b'Gevurah* is essential to us. We must open our mouths and be fed as we pass through this gate. We must fully take in the sweet and the savory offerings, so that we will live. This is not an optional gate. Do not pass it by. Love needs a good container, a channel through which to pour its joy, a cup with sides strong enough to overflow. Our days need doorways, and we need the discipline to enter them. Perhaps you can feel, or sense in some way, how firmly we are held in the communal counting, how surely and lightly we are turned? *Gevurah sh'b'Gevurah* is a dance well done. We grow from this turning.

Until tomorrow…

With love,

Susan/Shoshana Asiel

Dear One, spend some time today in quiet attention. Outdoors, if possible, just looking and listening. If a particular form invites you to look or listen longer—a petal, a naked branch, or an unfurling leaf, say—stay with that form, with soft eyes, noticing and appreciating its details with every sense. You may want to write or draw, or you may want to simply sit with senses open. It may be a quality of your own being that asks for your attention today. Whatever it is, spend some time with it, thanking yourself for whatever you are able to give and thanking the Source of All for what you are given.

Day 10
***Tiferet sh'b'Gevurah*: Compassion with Discipline**

(Eve of the 10th day, the third day of the second week of the *Omer*.)

bah'Ruch ah'Tah ahdoh'Nai, ehloh'Heynu Meh'lehch ha'oh'Lahm, ah'Shair k'd'Shahnu b'meetz'vo'Tahv, v'tzee'Vahnu Ahl s'fee'Raht hah'O'mer

> Blessed are You, God, Source of Strength and Power, You make us holy through Your *mitzvot*, commanding us to count the *Omer*.

ha'Yoam ah'sah'Rah yo'Meem, sh'Heym sha'Vooah
eh'Chod oo'shlo'Shah yah'Meem lah'O'mer

> Today is the tenth day of the *Omer*, which makes
> one week and three days of the *Omer*.

Ten days, Dear One, and still you are with me? This is
good. This is very, very good.

Beloveds,

Tiferet: Compassion, Harmony, Heartsong. Compassion
with discipline. Today we create a big space in the tent of
our hearts, making sure the tent-poles are firm. *Tiferet* is
broad vision, the wide angle lens of the heart, and *Tiferet*
has open, discerning ears. The finely tuned ear can hear the
harmonies within apparent cacophony; find the unity
among diverse voices. Within the gate of *Gevurah,* we pull
ourselves in, hold ourselves accountable by counting these
days. This particular day, the tenth day, I open to the
breadth of vision and depth of hearing that is *Tiferet*. To the
extent that I am able, I practice seeing with God's eyes,
hearing with God's ears.

Last year on the morning of *Tiferet sh'b'Gevurah*, I was on
a road-trip. Here is what I wrote:

> 8 AM, a rest stop on the Pennsylvania Turnpike: I
> look out the wall of window next to my table,
> beyond the empty chairs and glass topped tables on
> the patio to the line of tractor trailers and the
> Allegheny Mountains, rolling in blue and green

beyond. An unseasonably warm, mid-April Sunday morning—I am glad to be here, resting from the long drive behind and ahead, looking northward, taking in where I am now, what is, in this moment, true for me. All things are possible from here. I am going to Columbus, Ohio to be with a spiritual teacher who feeds me, but I don't want to miss this moment on the way.

I remembered the *Tiferet* lesson of another trip, another Sunday morning.

Provincetown Harbor, October Light

You
who would live in paradise
have you considered that paradise
lives in you?
Every day
a rose-gold blossom of the sun you love
rises in your chest
each second breaks
into a soft blue heaven
that spreads
everywhere you breathe
and the boats, distinct
luminous
hulls of every hue
at home now in their quiet
vertical yearning
rest in the center
of spacious circles

all boats
held together
in your harbor of harbors.

They are the longings
words unspoken but patiently rocking
in your breast
they are the smiles
irrepressibly gleaming within you
and every one you meet.

And I wrote on:

I turn and aim the wide angle of my heart to include
the scattering of people who are "resting" here, too,
at the tables on my side of the window: a dozen or
so travelers of all ages, sizes, and skin shades. I
notice the colors they wear: khaki shorts, lavender t-
shirt, rose-colored sari, navy windbreaker, blue
jeans, short pink skirt; I think about why they chose
them. Some wear baseball caps, some carry back
packs, some pocketbooks. Their faces—hard to find
the light there, but if my poem is true, the same sun
rises inside each of us. I focus on that for a moment
and begin to smile from the center of my forehead.
Look! A troop of Boy Scouts streams in through the
automatic door. I wonder where they are heading—
Gettysburg perhaps, that field of ghosts, and I look
at them with compassion for the lives they will lead,
lives that will hold, to be sure, triumph and blessing,
confusion and challenges awesome in years to
come. The boys do not see me. They do not notice
me praying for them, practicing *Tiferet*. Or is it
myself I pray for: *Let the doors of my heart open.*
Let me live more widely, love more.

As I prepared to write this piece today, I noticed in myself an inclination to shrink and withdraw from the task. There was tightness around the heart and a wish that I had never said I would do this, write these daily *Omer* messages. Why did I say I would? What if I have nothing of interest to say today? What if I embarrass myself, if I haven't already? It's too hard. It's too public. Takes too much time. What if the doors of my heart refuse to open one more crack?

Well, that's why we practice, I suppose—to get better at something that is difficult. And so I do practice. I sit here and write even though I do not want to. I listen a little deeper. I fumble along with my half-hearted song. I ask your forgiveness for my fumbling.

I pray for all of us: that we may take in the beauty of this day and all who walk therein, including, and most especially, ourselves.

Enjoy your day, beloveds.

With compassion for all,

Susan/Shoshana Asiel

Whew. What do you make of that, Dear One? I'm not sure what to make of myself here. I think the gates leading to *Tiferet* are difficult gates for me. We'll see how I fare in the weeks to come. It seems there is a part of myself that just doesn't want to open any wider than I already have, thank you very much. Well, there is some relief in saying that, as it was a relief to say it to my companions then. And here I am, still counting. And here you are. What's hard for you? Are there gates that trip you up? Scare you even? You may begin to notice patterns. Or perhaps not. Be curious. Take it all in.

Day 11
Netzach sh'b'Gevurah: **Purpose with Discipline**

(Eve of the 11th day, the fourth day of the second week of the *Omer*.)

bah'Ruch ah'Tah ahdoh'Nai, ehloh'Heynu Meh'lehch ha'oh'Lahm, ah'Shair k'd'Shahnu b'meetz'vo'Tahv, v'tzee'Vahnu Ahl s'fee'Raht hah'O'mer

> Blessed are You, God, Source of Strength and Power, You make us holy through Your *mitzvot*, commanding us to count the *Omer*.

ha'Yoam eh'Chod ah'Sahr yoam, sh'Heym sha'Vooah eh'Chod v'ahrbah'Ah yah'Meem lah'O'mer

> Today is the eleventh day of the *Omer*, which makes one week and four days of the *Omer*.

Hello again. Another day, another opening… May it be for a blessing.

Beloveds,

My heart cracked open today. What a relief! First of all, let me thank you, companions of my soul, for your many heartening messages. I continually receive your blessings. But before your messages, there was one from my older brother—it came in last night, just after I wrote my *Tiferet sh'b'Gevurah* message to you. As part of my current exploration of social media—Facebook, how to use it for holiness?—I have been creating a "fan page" for a performing ensemble I work with called Voices of a Different Dream, two poets and a singer who blend our voices in creative ways. The other night I took the initial step of inviting my current Facebook "friends" to become "fans" of Voices of a Different Dream. Facebook makes things like this easy—you just run through a list of your friends with their little pictures by their names and click on those you want to invite—another click and the thing is done. Many members of my family are on the list too. Since it is *Gevurah* week, I resisted the temptation to pass them by, or to select only a few. It's an old defense, keeping distance from my family of origin, expecting that they won't "get me" or won't want to "get me," so just ignoring them, passing right on by them. But this is *Gevurah* week and I am, after all, growing stronger, so I took myself in hand and invited everybody, even my big brother. It was the end of a long day, and I was tired. Yesterday evening's message to you had worn me out, and I was sure it wasn't good enough. But before bed, I did what I do lately before closing the computer: one final email check and a quick Facebook scan. The fans of Voices of a Different Dream have begun to gather, I noticed. But, wait a minute, look who is here on the screen! It's my older brother, his face, soft and grandfatherly now—I am not yet used to it. He has left this message:

> "I guess it's never too late to try to explore some deeper thoughts and feelings. I'd like to think that I might still be reachable."

I will not go into the family history that makes this message from my big brother so remarkable—you may imagine your own version. Suffice it to say that I was stunned. At the time, I couldn't fully take in the power of his post—I was just too tired. So I filed my brother's words and gentled face away for the morning. Then after a good night's sleep, waking up to the dawn of *Tiferet sh'b'Gevurah*, I could begin to take in the full beauty of what was offered, the sweetness of my brother's aging face, the simple clarity of his words. For my practice, I used one of Shefa's new chants, the one called "Sweet as Honey."[7] She wrote it for me because I've been drawn to the book of Ezekiel. I had asked her for a chant to go with the passage in which the prophet, in his encounter with "the appearance of the semblance of the Presence of the Lord," is handed a scroll and instructed by "the voice" to eat it.[8] On the scroll are the words: *KeeNeem, HeGeh*, and *Hee* (Lamentations, Dirges, and Woe). The prophet responds:

Va'ochlah va't'hi v'fi kidvash l'matok.

> I ate it, and it was in my mouth as sweet as honey.
> (Ezek 3:3)

I have loved those words since I first encountered them, in English, as a Methodist. Through my years as a Unitarian Universalist, I held on to the verse with a longing and a delight I could not explain. This morning I began spontaneously chanting the Hebrew in the shower, opening my mouth to receive the bitter and the sweet of my family story—through the ancient words, cradled in Shefa's new melody. I take it in; I taste and digest the whole thing—all that has happened in my family of origin, all that has not happened, all that is yet to be. I weep. In Philadelphia today, the uneasy April heat we've been having turned to a seasonally cool rain last night, and I am raining too. So good, so sweet. All of it.

For *Netzach sh'b'Gevurah,* I leave you with a poem, one I wrote for my favorite constellation, the Pleiades, visible in this part of the world in spring, summer and early fall. Most of the phrases are various names from different cultures for the star cluster that signals sailors when it's safe to set out on a long journey. "Blossoms of light" is from my sister poet, Ellen Mason of Voices of a Different Dream.[9]

Pleiades

Seven sisters.

Those who cluster and cling.

Dabs of paint. Brush strokes.

Lady of Heaven. Shining spoon.

Bunch of grapes. Hens and chicks.

Marketplace. Seed scatterers.

Flock of doves. Sparkling suns.

Stars of rain. Beneficent fire.

Blossoms of light.

Wind gatherers.

Orion's prey

Never caught.

My stars.

Sail on!

Netzach is the light that glimmers from afar. With practice, with *Gevurah*, *Netzach* helps us get where we need, and want, to go. Love the day as it comes to you.

Moving ever towards what we most desire,

I am your

Susan/Shoshana Asiel

When I get to *Netzach*, Dear One, I know I'm going to make it. It's an odd thing to say but seems true. And I imagine that when I get around to *Chesed*, *Hod*, and *Tiferet*, I'll again encounter some difficulties. So be it. Challenges purify the soul, so I am thinking now, from within the far-ranging wisdom of *Netzach* supported by the firm structure of *Gevurah*… Check the stars and moon today. Make a practice of tuning in to the guidance of the sky. See what you see there. Hear what you hear.

Day 12
Hod sh'b'Gevurah: Splendor, with Discipline

(Eve of the 12th day, the fifth day of the second week of the *Omer*.)

bah'Ruch ah'Tah ahdoh'Nai, ehloh'Heynu Meh'lehch ha'oh'Lahm, ah'Shair k'd'Shahnu b'meetz'vo'Tahv, v'tzee'Vahnu Ahl s'fee'Raht hah'O'mer

> Blessed are You, God, Source of Strength and Power, You make us holy through Your *mitzvot*, commanding us to count the *Omer*.

ha'Yoam sh'Nye'eem ah'Sahr yoam, sh'Heym sha'Vooah eh'Chod v'chah'mee'Shah yah'Meem lah'O'mer

Today is the twelfth day of the *Omer*, which makes one week and five days of the *Omer*.

Hello again, Dear One. Here we are at the gate of *Hod sh'b'Gevurah*. This day offers special treat: the discipline into which we are invited is the practice of pure delight. Enjoy…

Beloveds,

Earth today. Splendor of the everywhere ground. The stars are here—within, between, and among us. You can see them in the faces of the flowers we live with. Where we want to go is wherever we are, only more "here" than we've ever been before. I remember this flower from another season:

Morning Glory

There's a star on a vine
by the side of my house—
you can see it untwist
from a bud
tight as a pencil.
If you think the blue
of this unfolding glory
could make you stand
in one place forever,
wait until it opens—
wait until it twirls
inside out.

> There's a yellow in the well
> of the blue
> star's center—
> nothing will keep your face
> out of that flower.

The messages of *Hod* are simple, if not easy. I will leave
you today with this: Practice falling into the faces of the
flowers nearest you—all of them, not only the ones that
grow on stems and stalks. I must go now and do the same.

I love you.

Susan/Shoshana Asiel

Dear One, perhaps you have actual blossoms where
you live. Or perhaps not yet. No matter. See what's
around you, indoors and out. Take note: who is here in
your life—who are the ones who are near you?
Discreetly search their faces for a glint of starlight. Or
not so discreetly, if you dare. Once I was caught
looking at my obstreperous teenage son that way.
When he asked, defensively, why I was looking at
him, I told the truth: "Because you are beautiful." Or
perhaps I said "handsome," guessing the word would
land better on his ears, though it was far more than
handsome I was seeing. He looked away, but I saw the
glimmer of a smile, a hint of sweetness, around the
edges of his eyes and mouth.

Day 13
Yesod sh'b'Gevurah: **Foundation of Strength**

(Eve of the 13th day, the sixth day of the second week of
the *Omer*.)

*bah'Ruch ah'Tah ahdoh'Nai, ehloh'Heynu Meh'lehch
ha'oh'Lahm, ah'Shair k'd'Shahnu b'meetz'vo'Tahv,
v'tzee'Vahnu Ahl s'fee'Raht hah'O'mer*

> Blessed are You, God, Source of Strength and
> Power, You make us holy through Your *mitzvot*,
> commanding us to count the *Omer*.

*ha'Yoam sh'low'Shah ah'Sahr yoam, sh'Heym sha'Vooah
eh'Chod v'shee'Shah yah'Meem lah'O'mer*

> Today is the thirteenth day of the *Omer*, which
> makes one week and six days of the *Omer*.

Hello Dear One. How did you find the blossoms
around you? Did you remember to look into them? If
not, no worries—you can do this practice any moment
of your life, whenever you remember. Now on to a
different day…

Beloveds,

Our *Gevurah*, our strength, the ability to pull in around our
core and do the heavy lifting of life in a healthy way,
contains within it a fundamental sense of loyalty and faith,
qualities represented in the divine attribute *Yesod*. We

strengthen ourselves in order to be faithful to ourselves: to whom and to what we are. The gate of *Yesod* within *Gevurah* will not let us get away with a rigid sense of individual self—that would be no strength at all. This gate assures us that there is no 'I' without a 'we'—that each of us is born of and into relationship. There is simply no 'I' without 'you'. There is this endlessly intertwining God-dance: Us. We are betrothed, whether we know it or not, and our task is to come into the knowing, to live more and more fully into the enduring love that is our nature.

When I write a poem, the words don't begin to flow until I know to whom and for whom I am writing.

My Poetics

May I tell you a secret?
I wouldn't read poetry,
I certainly wouldn't write it,
if it weren't for you.

You are
what makes these words
worth it.

You're the value,
the pearl in them. Whoever you are,
you're the one I worship,
the one I seek when I go

plunging into the indigo deep

or when I roam the heaving seas
for what I lost or what I
hope to gain.

It's only you I want, only you
who sit there listening
at your little desk, waiting
in your perfect chair,
wanting, searching for
only me.

Thank you for being present to receive this flow. For my part, I will do my best to stay open.

All honor, all love is ours.

Gratefully,
Susan/Shoshana Asiel

Dear One,

How does it sit with you, this symbiotic relationship between us, between you and me and the starlight we are made of? Is it delicious, terrifying, confusing, thrilling, comforting? All of these and more, for me. Do you want to close the book now? Sometimes I do. But I don't, not for long anyway. Some days I think it is mostly my curiosity that keeps me going. How will it all turn out? What will be revealed to me next? If you're still with me, you've got a good measure of that too. Thank you for staying.

Day 14
Malchut sh'b'Gevurah: **Nobility with Judgment**

(Eve of the 14th day, the seventh day of the second week of the *Omer*.)

bah'Ruch ah'Tah ahdoh'Nai, ehloh'Heynu Meh'lehch
ha'oh'Lahm, ah'Shair k'd'Shahnu b'meetz'vo'Tahv,
v'tzee'Vahnu Ahl s'fee'Raht hah'O'mer

> Blessed are You, God, Source of Strength and
> Power, You make us holy through Your *mitzvot*,
> commanding us to count the *Omer*.

ha'Yoam ahr'bah'Ah ah'Sahr yoam, sh'Heym sh'Nay
sha'voo'Oat lah'O'mer

> Today is the fourteenth day of the *Omer*, which
> makes two weeks of the *Omer*.

Closing out the second week, Dear One… May the
blessings of *Shechina*, the indwelling spirit of the
Universe, be with you on this and every day.

Beloveds,

On the eve of *Malchut sh'b'Gevurah*, My Great Aunt Lena
comes to me. Sharing a household with my paternal
grandparents, she was a consistent and loving presence
throughout my childhood. I give her to you now:

Maiden Aunt

for LMD (1888-1969)

My Great Aunt
born Lena MacDonald Dunlap
teacher of eighth grade
English and Elocution
took her full name with her
to her grave.
It was her seal of birth
how could she discard
any piece of what she was most
grateful for?

Women all around her
married every day.
She did not judge them
but knew herself
she had made
a prior vow.

At sixteen, she fell from a handstand:
splintered her left leg.
Some say it was her lameness
some, an overbearing mother,
kept the men away.

She was the focus
of both parents' love.
When at twenty one,
she took a teaching post near New York
        City,
they sold the Shippensburg Hotel

and mother, father, sister, widowed aunt
all followed her
as if the sun itself
had relocated in the sky.

She had a teacher's way
of shedding light
and a singular gift of voice–
not so much the singing voice
as the clear tones of lucid speech–
she loved
the way a single word could toll
when uttered by a celebrating tongue
and word upon word
could call each listener
to love the world a little more.

She sought to find ways
to make her gifts resound
through the voice
of every stifled child she met.
This was her obligation
and her passion
for fifty years
in a Belleville, New Jersey
public school.
It was some years after she retired
I took my place in a captain's chair
beneath her amber lamp.
A third grade reader
opened in my lap
and whole, smooth sentences
rolled out of me in perfect waves
to break

upon her well-tuned ears.

If you can do that here
she said
you can do it
anywhere.

Malchut is leadership, majesty, nobility, integrity—that
which makes light shine through us, so that others can see a
bit better by virtue of our being. *Malchut* is the part of us
that envisions what's best for ourselves and for our
communities. *Malchut* is also called *Shechina*, indwelling
presence of the divine. The gate of *Shechina/Malchut*
within the gate of *Gevurah* offers us the discipline of
surrender: we choose, with exquisite good judgment, to
open to the divine flow that winds its way through all the
gates into us. Through *Shechina/Malchut* we give ourselves
to the glory of creation as it flows into and rises up out of
us—magnificent life! I imagine that my Aunt Lena, a
Methodist from a long line of same, didn't know much, if
anything at all, of Jewish mysticism. She lived her life
happily, with a grateful heart, a keen sense of fun, and a
commitment to helping others. I seem to need the company
of Jewish mystics for my happiness. I am glad to know this
now about myself. It is good to know what one needs. I
wonder who kept Lena Dunlap company in her deepest
places…

I honor my great aunt today and count her with us in these holy weeks, letting myself sink, with gratitude, into my roots, the beloved home of her bones.

Thank you for sharing this week with me. May the blessings of *Chesed* and *Gevurah*, kindness and good judgment, go with us as we travel on.

All love,

Susan/Shoshana Asiel

What do you find at the roots of your tree? Who shows up for you in this gate? Who are your guides, your supports, your loving companions, now and across the ages? Who keeps you company in your deepest places? What encourages and sustains your leadership? Which are the practices that help you move into the world with all your graces? Are you doing them? Take note. And dream well, Dear One. Dream well.

Week Three: *Tiferet*
Beauty, harmony, balance, compassion

Day 15
Chesed sh'b'Tiferet: **Kindness with Truth**

(Eve of the 15th day, the first day of the third week of the *Omer*.)

bah'Ruch ah'Tah ahdoh'Nai, ehloh'Heynu Meh'lehch ha'oh'Lahm, ah'Shair k'd'Shahnu b'meetz'vo'Tahv, v'tzee'Vahnu Ahl s'fee'Raht hah'O'mer

> Blessed are You, God, Source of Harmony, You make us holy through Your *mitzvot*, commanding us to count the *Omer*.

ha'Yoam chahmee'Shah a'Sahr yoam, sh'Heym shnay shahvoo'Oat v'Yoam eh'Chod lah'O'mer

> Today is fifteen days, which is two weeks and one day of the *Omer*.

Hello Dear One,

Welcome to week three. This is heart-medicine week. Begin now returning to the practice of heart awareness, gently breathing in and around that most amazing and sustaining organ—shoulders up, back and down, creating space in the chest and back for the heart to do its vital work. Remember to do this often in the course of all your days, but especially this week, as we move through the gate of *Tiferet*. The gate itself will help you remember, if you remember to let it.

Beloveds,

Today begins the week of *Tiferet*: the gate of compassion, harmony, truth. *Tiferet* is the wide-angle lens of the heart. *Tiferet* makes music, integrates a diversity of voices into one song, beautiful and true. In *Tiferet*, we hold the truth with reverence, accepting what is so with grace. *Tiferet* balances *Chesed* and *Gevurah*—holding in equal measure the flow of loving-kindness and the ability to set appropriate boundaries. *Tiferet* offers a wide open "yes" to love and delight and a firm, assured "no" to self-indulgence.

And today we come around again to *Chesed*, the pearl we are given at birth and which we find again and again when we need it. *Chesed* is the ability to love and be loved completely and unconditionally—the unstoppable flow of the human heart, the milk of our souls, the basic nurturance that makes our lives possible. *Chesed* is channeled through the human form, through no other beings but us.

When I was three, sometimes I was allowed to take my afternoon nap on my mother's bed. This was an awesome privilege.

My Mother Sleeping

She who lies beside me
is the mountain I have not grown into.
See how enormously she sleeps
beneath our shared blanket.

My tiny body, without breasts, with only
small points for knees
barely disturbs
the broad plain of her bed.
Her body rises magnificently from her throat
and rolls, rolls, rolls
to the far away valley of her feet.

I cannot sleep
for the depths of my worship.
I keep my eyes open
to the lift and fall
of her every breath.
She has dropped the morning paper
like a tent across her belly–
I wish I could be a word
on that page. Maybe then
maybe then she would read me–
maybe then I could enter

her dreams.

Now, ten years after my mother's death, I think perhaps I
have entered her dream, a love-dream. Perhaps my heart is
growing wide enough to contain my mother's love—my
love for her, her love for her children. Perhaps I have
grown up enough to do this.

I went to see my sister today—my monthly visit. Instead of
taking her to lunch as my friend and I had planned, I ended
up in an emergency meeting with her psychiatrist, social
worker, and therapist at the mental health agency that

coordinates her care, while my friend stayed in the waiting room. My sister's helpers are warm, kind, and competent. But things are not going well for Meg right now. In the psychiatrist's office, having just learned disturbing news about her recent, risky sexual behaviors, my heart caved; no doubt I sank a bit in my chair. I saw the kindness in the eyes of the social worker as she sent me a look that said *I know. It's terrifying. I feel it too.* And then the *Malchut* of our Great Aunt Lena came to lift me from my slump. Ten years my junior, Meg was too young to know Aunt Lena very well. I was the lucky one. My mother, after marrying my father, was to become herself a beloved niece of Aunt Lena. I sensed then that I/we live inside the love of those who have come before us; my brothers, sister, and I live now inside our mother's love. The mother, whose death eleven years ago devastated us, lives and loves through us now. It's a wonder. Anything can happen, I thought, in the light of such love. And I hear my mother's voice: *There is no end to this love.* Unending love, Great love. *Ahava Raba.* My sister cannot take in the *Chesed* that surrounds her. In truth, she pushes it away, but I can take it in. And I can love my sister with a wide love, a great, heart-rending love. My mother's dream can take us from there.

Love well, love widely, beloved ones.

Receive every kindness that comes your way.

Shoshana Asiel

Are there places, situations in your life, Dear One, that need the wide-angle lens of the heart? Where is your loving most challenged, where your compassion is needed? What do you most wish were not true about yourself or someone else? If something comes to mind now, take note, and know that the medicine of *Tiferet* is available to you, as near to you as heart and breath.

Day 16
Gevurah sh'b'Tiferet: Awe within Compassion

(Eve of the 16th day, the second day of the third week of the *Omer*.)

bah'Ruch ah'Tah ahdoh'Nai, ehloh'Heynu Meh'lehch ha'oh'Lahm, ah'Shair k'd'Shahnu b'meetz'vo'Tahv, v'tzee'Vahnu Ahl s'fee'Raht hah'O'mer.

> Blessed are You, God, Source of Harmony, You make us holy through Your *mitzvot*, commanding us to count the *Omer*.

ha'Yoam shee'Shah a'Sahr yoam, sh'Heym shnay shahvoo'Oat oo'Shnay yah'Meem lah'O'mer

> Today is the sixteenth day of the *Omer*, which is two weeks and two days of the *Omer*.

Are you remembering to practice your heart awareness, Dear One? In our culture it is so easy to forget. Here I am to remind you...

Beloveds,

"Receive every kindness that comes your way." It seemed a strange thing for me to leave you with last night, but those were the words that came, and I needed a closing line, so I let them be. Sometimes I feel the kindness of others will break me, especially when I am frightened and pulled in around myself. Yesterday a dear friend had come along for the visit to my sister. In the car after the meeting, when my friend's hand reached to comfort me, my own hand snapped back. I couldn't take the kindness. That is the way my sister lives—continually retracting from a world that is frightening to her. I suppose her way is an extreme reflection of my own, how I can be when terrified, especially when trying to behave as if I am not.

My Faith

Forgive me if my terror shows.
Forgive me, if it doesn't.

Inside is a fear
so great and nameless
I can barely stand here
at your door.

If you find me on my knees,
please understand.
There is something I need
from the stone at your feet.

If I quake but do not bend,
help me down.
There is ground
I know will hold,

this wavering soul.

So what am I afraid of? *Gevurah sh'b'Tiferet*. Awe within compassion, the awe of compassion, is close to the fear of compassion. In Hebrew "fear" and "reverence" are the same word. The two meanings together make our English "awe." Perhaps trembling is the natural response of a small and thoughtful creature to the vastness of the Mystery in which we move, a mystery that seems somehow to love us—so our scriptures tell us and so has been my experience—but a mystery in which we are ultimately and thoroughly consumed. When I gave birth to my son, I trembled for hours afterwards. I am told that many women do this. If fear/reverence/awe is the beginning of wisdom, as the Hebrew Scriptures tell us more than once, perhaps it is so because it brings us trembling to our knees—closer to the ground of which we are made and from which, with help, we rise, when the little casings of our separate selves are broken open.

Not much else to say tonight—think I'll just tremble on to bed…

With gratitude for your continually kind messages to me in response to these writings and in awe of your presence in my life

I am

yours

With love,

Shoshana Asiel

And for your presence too, Dear One, I am grateful. Be open to the peculiar blessings of the day. Whatever surprises come your way, practice receiving them as blessings, even if they do not at first appear so. Be curious about the blessings hidden within every experience. Spend a little time on your knees.

Day 17
Tiferet sh'b'Tiferet: **Heart of Compassion**

(Eve of the 17th day, the third day of the third week of the *Omer*.)

bah'Ruch ah'Tah ahdoh'Nai, ehloh'Heynu Meh'lehch ha'oh'Lahm, ah'Shair k'd'Shahnu b'meetz'vo'Tahv, v'tzee'Vahnu Ahl s'fee'Raht hah'O'mer.

> Blessed are You, God, Source of Harmony, You make us holy through Your *mitzvot*, commanding us to count the *Omer*.

ha'Yoam shee'Vah a'Sahr yoam, sh'Heym shnay shahvoo'Oat oo'shlo'Shah yah'Meem lah'O'mer

Today is the seventeenth day of the *Omer*, which is
two weeks and three days of the *Omer*.

Dear One, are you ready to open your heart wider than
you think you can? Wider than you may want? Is there
a part of you that shouts, "No! Wait! Slow down!"? If
so, that's good news, because it is good to move very
slowly through these days, savoring every turn. And if
you are ready to roll your shoulders back and spread
those wings, well, then, do.

Beloveds,

Welcome to the essence of *Tiferet*: the core, the heart of the
Universe, the very pith of our being.

Human

Do not be frightened when beauty strikes
though it leaves you mute and sleepless
churning and roiling like a sea
struck by some sudden turn of wind.
It is only the sun that does this—
the source of light plays
through the atmosphere and changes
everything it touches, always.

If this is happening to you in some violent
     way
threatening your very core
if beauty feels more blade than blessing
your life more blood than stone

be glad in your grief you are human
grateful for the liquid in your pith—lean

into the beauty that never leaves you
the only life that truly lights you.

Tiferet within *Tiferet* is the intelligent, measured music at
the core of our being, the pulse we share with all that lives,
the light that is ours to absorb and reflect. Through this
gate, we gather extra energy and courage. We expand our
hearts. Doors open within doors, showing us the widest
possible horizon. We can use this extra energy to be
compassionate with the most difficult people, the most
troublesome parts of ourselves, and the most painful
situations in the world. *Tiferet*, the attribute that integrates
Chesed and *Gevurah*, brings love and fear together, yoking
them in the human heart. With the heart's expansive love
and courage, we can transform these energies into
unimaginable acts of healing and justice. A Benedictine
teacher of mine once taught me that courage pre-supposes
fear. Our true strength is born of our ability to tremble. And
when our sense of mercy works together with our
tremulous courage, we move ever more deeply into our true
being. The doors of our hearts fling wide today to receive
the essential beauty of the cosmos in its manifold forms.
From this we live.

I find myself at the gate of *Tiferet* once again with gratitude
and relief for the pleasures of an open heart. I live more
securely in the knowledge of who I am, who we are, and

what is unfolding within, among, and between us. Today was the third Thursday of the month. Along with a thousand or so Jews and allies I participate in *Ta'anit Tzadek*, the Fast for Gaza, a monthly fast called forth by a consortium of rabbis and other clerics, to pray in solidarity with the people of Gaza. I skipped breakfast, donned my *Kippah* for the day, along with a button—"American Jews for a Just Peace"— and went to my synagogue at 7:30 AM. My rabbi and I sat together, chanting and breathing silently, reflecting a bit on the terrible realities of this war and how it is that we sit here praying, holding the door open for the unimaginable. Knowing that others across the country and world are doing something like this on the same day brings us a profound sense of hope, a sense of the earth and the people of the earth growing, however slowly, toward what we most want and need: *Shalom v'Tzadik*, peace and justice.

Tiferet sh'b'Tiferet, day of the open heart, a day of the deepest, widest opening, is a day of the greatest hope. I am glad to be with you on this most auspicious day.

All love,

Shoshana Asiel

Dear One, this is a good day to spread your wings, enjoy the span. Ask yourself, where is the strength and breadth of my love most needed on this day? Go there. If this feels too difficult, or somehow not quite the

right time, then return to the gentle heart-breath
practice and bring that soft awareness also to your
shoulder blades, the base of your wings. Love them as
they are.

Day 18
Netzach sh'b' Tiferet: **Persistence in Compassion**

(Eve of the 18th day, the fourth day of the third week of the
Omer.)

*bah'Ruch ah'Tah ahdoh'Nai, ehloh'Heynu Meh'lehch
ha'oh'Lahm, ah'Shair k'd'Shahnu b'meetz'vo'Tahv,
v'tzee'Vahnu Ahl s'fee'Raht hah'O'mer.*

> Blessed are You, God, Source of Harmony, You
> make us holy through Your *mitzvot*, commanding us
> to count the *Omer*.

*ha'Yoam sh'Moanah a'Sahr yoam, sh'Heym shnay
shahvoo'Oat v'ar'bah'Ah yah'Meem lah'O'mer*

> Today is the eighteenth day of the *Omer*, which is
> two weeks and four days of the *Omer*.

Dear One, I love arriving at the gate of *Netzach*, the
gate of endurance and long vision. Today is the
eighteenth day; eighteen is a number of special
blessing, according to the mystics: the Hebrew letters
of the word *Chai* (life) are the numerical equivalents of
the number eighteen. Will you join me in taking a
moment here to appreciate how far we've come

together? And in the next moment cast a glance at the trail ahead in this journey of forty-nine days. Enjoy yourself now, moving rhythmically along, day in, day out, within and toward divine revelation, always present and yet to come. Here are some lines from the evening liturgy to keep you company: *Golel Or meepNay Choshech, Choshech meepNay Or,* "Rolling away light before darkness, darkness before light…"

Beloveds,

Welcome to the gate of *Netzach* within *Tiferet*. Here we encounter our ability to follow through on the impulses of our open hearts, our capacity to persist in the life of compassion, though the doors of our hearts will close, though we will sometimes shrink from the enormity of the needs around us. The challenge, the invitation, the calling, the beckoning of *Netzach sh'b'Tiferet* is to keep moving along our narrow and serpentine path in beauty, toward beauty.

As far as I can see, we are heading toward a way of living on earth that manifests the intimate, daily knowing of our interdependence—the incomparably sweet experience of knowing that we are diverse entities within one glorious Self. Once I heard Reb Zalman Schachter-Shalomi, sage of Jewish Renewal, say that if we practiced an awareness of ourselves as a single cell in the earth's body for five minutes a day, for 40 consecutive days, we would understand how to live. We would begin to manifest daily the exquisite connected-ness that is the truth of our being. A habit, he said, takes about 40 days to nestle in. I tried the practice last year at this time, lost track after five days, started over, forgot again after 10 days and haven't remembered until now.

My notes from last year tell this:

> Today, on *Netzach sh'b'Tiferet,* I am off to an elementary school in Northeast Philadelphia to teach 100 5th and 6th grade public school students about the uses of poetry. It is not a well-run school—the classes are too large, the native languages of the students are many, the teachers for the most part overwhelmed and under supported. The children's education revolves around how high or low they will score on the standardized tests that will determine the school's annual progress, tests that have no apparent relationship to the children's lives. We are part of an experiment to see whether teaching artists, with our creative ways, can help raise the test scores. So many children, so many needs, such a dysfunctional and misguided system… I could easily be overwhelmed—and sometimes I am. But *Netzach* raises my head and keeps my eye on the prize; *Tiferet* helps my heart open to the beauty of the children's lives and the teachers who struggle to teach them. There is one class in particular that keeps me hopeful. It is the one in the trailer, set apart from the noisy halls of the main building, with a class kept small because of the trailer's size, and a young teacher who is wired for love.

A Poet's Visit

This wind I bring
this bowl of breath I am
wends its way to you
through mysterious hands—
I don't know what brought me here
I know only that I land
in the school yard and whirl
into your trailer, Fifth Grade Class!
Your slender box trembles
with every February gust
and the frantic scurry of squirrels
on a roof that hasn't yet
blown off.

Be safe, beloveds,
children of all the nations.
Hunger is swirling all about us
and there are wars that haven't yet begun.
Be fed, in this closed and quiet space, open
to what for certain nourishes.
Refuse, keep out,
what does not come to you with love.
Grow strong in your choices:
pick your best, most powerful words.
Use them with care—
create the world
we want.

Ethan Allen School, 2009

Keep your heads up, beloveds—eyes on the prize! Refuse what does not come to you with love.

Persistently yours,

Shoshana Asiel

Dear One, did you notice that I have begun to sign my name differently, leaving off the English name? This practice of counting and attending to the gates is building strength and confidence; it seems, in the prophetic voice, my prophetic voice, the truth that comes, in its particular way, through me. I am becoming more at ease with who I sense myself to be. How are you with your prophetic voice? The gate of *Netzach* in the gate of Truth is a fine place to take stock.

Day 19
Hod sh'b' Tiferet: Humility within Beauty

(Eve of the 19th day, the fifth day of the third week of the *Omer*.)

bah'Ruch ah'Tah ahdoh'Nai, ehloh'Heynu Meh'lehch ha'oh'Lahm, ah'Shair k'd'Shahnu b'meetz'vo'Tahv, v'tzee'Vahnu Ahl s'fee'Raht hah'O'mer.

> Blessed are You, God, Source of Harmony, You make us holy through Your *mitzvot*, commanding us to count the *Omer*.

ha'Yoam tee'Shah a'Sahr yoam, sh'Heym shnay
shahvoo'Oat va'chahmee'Shah yah'Meem lah'O'mer

> Today is the nineteenth day of the *Omer*, which is
> two weeks and five days of the *Omer*.

Here we are at *Hod* again. Ready to kiss the earth?

Beloveds,

Ahhh… It is good to arrive at the gate of *Hod sh'b'Tiferet*.
I experience the energies of this gate in a gesture—arms
flung wide, open heart, head thrown back, throat open to
the glory of creation in all of its wildness—then bowing,
bending from the knees, touching forehead to earth. *Hod*
folds me into the place from which I grow: the particular
beauty of being me, my unique, cellular reality. Here I
know my place in the breathing body of the Great Love.
Where I breathe is exactly where I belong.

Reflection

> These hemlock boughs bending low
> over the jade water
> will not give up on me,
> no matter how long it takes
> to understand
> the words of this love.
> Green to green forever leaning,
> the beauty of their form
> given back to them
> from the liquid depths.

Of course, they do not see this—
they do not need to.
Nor do they know the space between
the river's limpid skin
and the branches' feathered touch
is a holy place, where none
but the breezes enter
and perhaps
the smallest wings.

All I can do really with my little pulse is to receive the
messages I get and send the messages I must—all for the
health of the One who holds and contains us. That's why I
exist. So simple. But it is never easy to be simple. I take my
turn through the humble, yet splendid gate of *Hod
sh'b'Tiferet*, learn to listen with care to the spaces between
us and hear the harmonies of the universe.

Bowing to you, beloveds,

Shoshana Asiel

I find myself wondering, Dear One, whether everyone
loves the gate of *Hod* as much as I do. I suppose we
each have our preferences, and our resistances… I, for
instance, am deliciously at ease in *Hod*—comfortable
with praise, splendor, adoration. But if I were not
attentive in the gates that are more challenging for me,
if I didn't watch my step in the difficult dance of
Chesed and *Gevurah*, love and boundaries, and work
the balance of the two in *Tiferet*, attending reverently
to the heart muscle, I might arrive in *Netzach* and *Hod*

unprepared for the struggle between the two. I might be rigid and overly attached to outcome in *Netzach*, and dreamily self-indulgent in *Hod*. Left to my own devices, I am perfectly capable of each. At some point, if you have not already done so, it would be good to notice your predilections and discomforts, so that, alert and informed, you may continue to keep yourself good company on this journey. You may use the energy of this week of *Tiferet* to learn some truth that you may not have recognized before about yourself and your patterns. For whatever you discover, say thank you.

Day 20
Yesod sh'b' Tiferet: **Commitment with Compassion**

(Eve of the 20th day, the sixth day of the third week of the *Omer*.)

bah'Ruch ah'Tah ahdoh'Nai, ehloh'Heynu Meh'lehch ha'oh'Lahm, ah'Shair k'd'Shahnu b'meetz'vo'Tahv, v'tzee'Vahnu Ahl s'fee'Raht hah'O'mer.

> Blessed are You, God, Source of Harmony, You make us holy through Your *mitzvot*, commanding us to count the *Omer*.

ha'Yoam ehs'Reem yoam, sh'Heym shnay shahvoo'Oat v'shee'Shah yah'Meem lah'O'mer

> Today is the twentieth day of the *Omer*, which is two weeks and six days of the *Omer*.

Dear One, are you noticing your patterns? Perhaps not yet… No matter. Carry on with love.

Beloveds,

Yesod sh'b'Tiferet: Commitment in Compassion… Bonding with Beauty… Holding of Harmony… *Yesod* integrates the energies of *Hod* and *Netzach*, bringing together into one body the one who stands still to praise with the one who moves on toward the distant lights. *Yesod* provides the structure for *Tiferet's* open heart, a strong channel for the heart's flow.

This morning I took part in an Earth Day Celebration at a local church in which I was a solo speaking voice— offering poetry between the choir's hymns to the earth. My voice supported the glory of the songs. This is a Unitarian Universalist community to which I have been committed for a long time. Pulling away from the congregation has not been easy and has taken time. Though I am Jewish now and attend synagogue more regularly than church, still, in the spirit of *Yesod*, I honor my long-term relationship with this community, as I acknowledge also that the relationship has changed. I am no longer involved in the week to week running of the congregation, nor am I a regular attendee—I return now for special visits like this one.

I can bring the congregation something of my Jewish life now, as I did today—attention to the cycles of the moon, for instance, and an evolving intimacy with ancient text, through regular exposure and on-going commitment. This weekly relationship to scripture is something I had missed in Unitarian Universalist worship.

Reading Ezekiel under the Moon

Take any text—
any word, any letter,
any sound to its source,
you will find me, waiting.
I am waiting for you forever.

Take the simple sound of *z*, for instance.
Let it be a crown for you.
Wear it like the open circle of the moon
over you always in your travels.
Month after month,
see how she strengthens—helps you
remember your birth, the exact nature
of your lineage
and what you have to do with it.

Take your time. Time is what I give you,
what I want you to have: your entire life
enmeshed, imbued
with the holiness of hours.
Do not hurry the words.
They are hidden, for a purpose,
in the book of your sorrows,
in the legends of your nights and days.

Take any text, any letter, any sound,
any fire at all—whatever you find

inscribed in your heart's open doors
and follow it, a thread
cerulean from the source
to the river's mouth.

Then, there, knee-deep in these wetlands,
you may speak.

Oh and yes, a rich sense of the holiness of time... Judaism
has fed me that. If I hadn't moved on from the place where
I had been celebrating, I wouldn't have been able to return
to the community to embody that holiness, as I could today.
How wondrous, these cerulean threads—look where they
take us, see where we land, and with what treasure in our
hands!

For the beauty of the earth

I am

yours

with love,

Shoshana Asiel

This could be a good time to pick up the threads of
your spiritual journey and hold them in your fingers
with loving attention. Here are some questions you
may ask. Use what's helpful; disregard the rest. When
did you first know you were a spiritual being, that you
were more than the sum of your parts? Where did that
knowledge first take you? What traditions have you

explored? Have you landed in any particular religion? What practices have you picked up along the way? What have you dropped? What communities and experiences have most nourished your soul? Where are you now and how did you get here? To what traditions or practices are you drawn now? Give an appreciative look, with an enduring love for the mysterious unfolding that is your life.

Day 21
Malchut sh'b'Tiferet: **Integrity with Compassion**

(Eve of the 21st day, the seventh day of the third week of the *Omer*.)

bah'Ruch ah'Tah ahdoh'Nai, ehloh'Heynu Meh'lehch ha'oh'Lahm, ah'Shair k'd'Shahnu b'meetz'vo'Tahv, v'tzee'Vahnu Ahl s'fee'Raht hah'O'mer.

> Blessed are You, God, Source of Harmony, You make us holy through Your *mitzvot*, commanding us to count the *Omer*.

ha'Yoam eh'Chod v'ehs'Reem yoam, sh'Heym sh'lo'Shah shahvoo'Oat lah'O'mer

> Today is the twenty-first day of the *Omer*, which is three weeks of the *Omer*.

Dear One, if you are not familiar with Hebrew, I will teach you a good word. The word is *Hineni*. It means "Here I am." The Jews I know, including this one, use

it to say "I am present, here, in this moment and ready
to be used for a good purpose."

Beloveds,

I woke today with a twinge of fear, a sense of wanting to
run from something, to pull my blankets over my head and
hide from the day. Today was fifteen years since the act of
homegrown terrorism that destroyed the Oklahoma City
Federal Building and the people within. The news these
days is full of anti-government rage and racial hatred thinly
disguised as political righteousness. I sense in the air
around me a nervousness that something like the massacre
perpetrated by Timothy McVeigh could happen again, any
minute. From within the gate of *Malchut sh'b' Tiferet*, the
can-do gate of compassion and beauty, I offer a standing
prayer. I mean it as an antidote to terror, and a prayer for
healing, the growing health and maturation of our culture.

Hineni

I'm here. I'll stay.
I say it from the edge of a dream.
Meaning... I'm not sure what...
meaning that
with you is the way
I want to be,
the way I am and have
always been.
I learn this, turning
in the spaces between

night and day, awake
and miraculously joined
in the illuminated abyss
through which we move
every moment of our lives
and from which all
our hours are created, blessed:
made good enough to let go, to release
into the firmament,
come what will.

Hineni. What do I mean with my new vow?
Here I am. Here I stay.
It's something a little different from
what I've promised before. I feel it
in the molecules of my bones,
how they swirl more lightly
and with a smile, how their spinning
settles me into sleep, the rest I
do surely, do sorely need
since I am to do the work
of making the world every minute
a luminous place.

I'll stay.
I'll stay with you
because I cannot do the work alone.
What you ask, what you want is
ours to do: our creation,
our unfolding world. I understand.
Hineni. I hear you and am
steadied, stayed, standing
in your light.

Good night. Or good morning. Whenever, wherever this finds you, love-lights, may it find you well.

Hineni.

Shoshana Asiel

Well, Dear One, I have been consistently now, all week long, "Shoshana Asiel." Where is the "Susan" I began with? I expected to keep my two names present throughout the weeks. I had a good reason for it. But something else is happening to me. Something I had not planned. I am not, however, ready to speak about it, just to notice.

What is happening with you? What do you notice? Is there something, perhaps, stirring within you that is not ready to be spoken? Some truths will be perfectly clear as in my "*Hineni*"—Here I Am. Some will be still shifting and forming. As we close this our third week together through the gates, honor both the clear knowingness and the subterranean stirrings. Many blessings!

Week Four: *Netzach*
Endurance, victory, physical energy, persistence

Day 22
Chesed sh'b'Netzach: **Love with Persistence**

(Eve of the 22nd day, the 1st day of the fourth week of the *Omer*.)

*bah'Ruch ah'Tah ahdoh'Nai, ehloh'Heynu Meh'lehch
ha'oh'Lahm, ah'Shair k'd'Shahnu b'meetz'vo'Tahv,
v'tzee'Vahnu Ahl s'fee'Raht hah'O'mer.*

> Blessed are You, God, Source of Endurance, You make us holy through Your *mitzvot*, commanding us to count the *Omer*.

*ha'Yoam sh'Nai'eem v'ehs'Reem yoam, sh'Heym
sh'low'Shah shahvoo'Oat v'Yoam eh'Chod lah'O'mer.*

> Today is the twenty-second day of the *Omer*, which is three weeks and one day of the *Omer*.

Dear One, if you feel your energy for the day by day counting flagging a bit in this fourth week, not to worry. It's natural. This is a long haul, and we're approaching the middle of the journey. Take heart. Be kind to yourself. Accept your distractions with good humor. And resume.

Beloveds,

I am preparing to travel this weekend for a presentation to a Unitarian Universalist congregation outside Richmond, Virginia. I will talk and read poems about my "convergence" with Judaism, a talk which I have yet to put together. As it turns out this week of *Netzach* is the week I first "shepherded" for my smaller *Kol Zimra* community in 2008, the twenty-seven intimates of my own class before we joined the larger groups of graduates. I wasn't Jewish yet, though plans for my ceremony of "convergence" were underway. This week I will let my younger self carry on for me. I apologize if the time warp is in any way discordant for you. It is with kindness towards self that I post these messages as I wrote them then, without tinkering—if I begin to rework them I will never get done what I must do this week. Here we go…

May 11, 2008

Beloved Wanderers,

Today begins week four, twenty-two days, which are three weeks and one day, of the *Omer*. I am your good shepherd of the week of *Netzach*, the week of Perseverance, Victory, Endurance. I am completely new to this practice and approach my duties humbly, with fresh eyes, open heart, and a willingness to persist.

I am drawn to the dictionary. In the ancient root of the word *netzach*, I found this: "to glitter from afar, to be eminent, permanent; the bright object at a distance traveled toward; splendor, truthfulness, confidence." This gate invites us to move with confidence toward that which beckons us, however distantly, however foggily. It's a strong light, a constant star. And so are we. And so we must become for others, especially for those exiled parts

of ourselves. We are called to simply stand and
shine, stand and welcome, even as we travel great
distances to find our way.

The daily practice I suggest for this week is the
chant *Elecha Yah Ekra*—To You, God, I Call
(Psalm 30: 9).[10] This verse can cover the distance
needed to help us get back home. I suggest chanting
this once a day all week long—to persevere in our
calling and in our listening.

This day is *Chesed* of *Netzach*, and so we are
invited to move with loving-kindness toward all our
goals.

Here is a poem to keep us company. I will send you
a poem every day this week, along with a few
thoughts in prose.

How Some People Move

for Cathy Cohen

Some people move through the world
with a softness so powerful
you have to slow down
to listen.
Some people move
like a poem
the kind you remember
keep close to you your whole life
the poem that's there when you need it
like the nourishment of your mother, father
or whoever it was that fed you
when you needed to be fed.

Some people learn to live
by listening
beneath the noise of people and things
to the quiet calling
and in their listening learn
to tremble.
Some people become themselves
the hum of the world
so soft, so powerful
you have to slow down to listen.

All love,

Susan/Shoshana Asiel

So that was my first day as an *Omer* shepherd. How readily I took up my new Hebrew name! There it is, "Shoshana Asiel" right alongside "Susan." I believe this was the first time I ever used it. Do you think it curious that I volunteered to lead before I knew what the *Omer* was? I do. I do not usually step into leadership so quickly, without hesitation. But there was something glimmering for me in the distance, some brightness I sensed was with me, though far off. Have you had experiences like this? Times when you agreed to do something that seemed both right and ridiculous at once? Perfect and impossible? Completely natural and totally unexpected? As I grow older, my life becomes more and more dappled with these experiences. This delights me.

Day 23
Gevurah sh'b'Netzach: **Strength with Persistence**

(Eve of the 23rd day, the second day of the fourth week of the *Omer*.)

*bah'Ruch ah'Tah ahdoh'Nai, ehloh'Heynu Meh'lehch
ha'oh'Lahm, ah'Shair k'd'Shahnu b'meetz'vo'Tahv,
v'tzee'Vahnu Ahl s'fee'Raht hah'O'mer.*

> Blessed are You, God, Source of Endurance, You
> make us holy through Your *mitzvot*, commanding us
> to count the *Omer*.

*ha'Yoam sh'low'Sheem v'ehs'Reem yoam, sh'Heym
sh'low'Shah shahvoo'Oat v'Shnay ya'Meem lah'O'mer.*

> Today is the twenty-third day of the *Omer*, which is
> three weeks and two days of the *Omer*.

Carrying on, toward love, with love…

Continuing, from 2008:

> May 12, 2008

> Beloved Wanderers—

> Today is twenty-three days, which are three weeks
> and two days of the *Omer*. Having entered the
> larger gate of *Netzach*, Perseverance, we stand now
> within the smaller gate of *Gevurah*, Restraint. What
> might it mean to exercise restraint, even as we
> persist in moving toward our destination?

Determined to find our way home, we must yet be
still and steady ourselves. We must make conscious,
considered choices about when we move, where,
and how, so that we find ourselves in the places and
the times just right for us. When we are doing the
right thing, in the right time and place, our light
shines strong, and others can see by the strength of
our beam. A light that flickers and flits, or races on
ahead of the caravan is not helpful to the journeyers.

So perhaps the energy of *Gevurah sh'b'Netzach* is
something like this poem I wrote five years ago, on
the eve of the outbreak of the Iraq War, when one
hundred and seven others and I blocked the
entrances to the Federal Building in Philadelphia in
protest. There were many such acts of civil
disobedience throughout the nation on that day.

The News

When you live
inside of lies
let yourself burn.
Your flame
is a strong cord
deep within,
you are lit
by a fire
not entirely
your own.
You're the glow
in the clouded glass.
Soft and sure
and steady

you must stay
in the one place
knowing
you will be seen
by those who seek
light
in this obfuscated land.

March 20, 2003

When I feel pulled, driven, obsessed or distracted
by thoughts of too much to do or too many places to
be, it is a good time to be still, to gather my
scattered selves and shine. *Elecha Yah Ekra*. It's a
good time to practice my calling.

To you, God, I call
with love,
Susan/Shoshana Asiel

This would be a good day, Dear One, to take stock of
the general direction of your life. Where are you
heading? Is it the direction that feels right for now?
What do you see in the distance? If you feel that a
change of direction is in order and don't know where
to turn, spend some time in meditation, breathing with
the words *Elecha Yah Ekra* (To you, Breath of Life, I
call). Send your call out to the far side of the horizon,
and listen for the call that returns. Meditate this way as
often as you can this week. Once a day would be ideal.
If this practice doesn't work for you, try something
else. If you experience resistance to practicing

anything at all, ask for help from the good gate of
Gevurah. Take note, and be grateful for everything
received.

Day 24
Tiferet sh'b'Netzach: Compassion with Persistence

(Eve of the 24rd day, 3rd day of the fourth week of the
Omer.)

*bah'Ruch ah'Tah ahdoh'Nai, ehloh'Heynu Meh'lehch
ha'oh'Lahm, ah'Shair k'd'Shahnu b'meetz'vo'Tahv,
v'tzee'Vahnu Ahl s'fee'Raht hah'O'mer.*

> Blessed are You, God, Source of Endurance, You
> make us holy through Your *mitzvot*, commanding us
> to count the *Omer*.

*ha'Yoam ar'bah'Ah v'ehs'Reem yoam, sh'Heym
sh'low'Shah shahvoo'Oat v'sh'low'Sheem ya'Meem
lah'O'mer.*

> Today is the twenty-fourth day of the *Omer*, which
> is three weeks and three days of the *Omer*.

Dear One, coming around to *Tiferet* again. Isn't it
lovely to circle round and round again to beauty,
harmony, balance, truth? Do you know that this gate is
always present, always waiting for us?

Continuing from 2008:

May 13, 2008

Beloveds—

Today is twenty-four days, which are three weeks and three days, of the *Omer*. This is the gate of *Tiferet sh'b'Netzach*. *Tiferet* is associated with compassion, harmony, and beauty, the center of the Tree of Life. Exploring the ancient root of *Tiferet* leads me to "beautify, ornament, glorify." I was confused by the association of such an inner, heart word (compassion) with the more visual connotations I found in the lexicon. But perhaps it is just my western mind that is confused. Beauty, in the ancient Middle Eastern mindset, would have shown from the inside out and the outside would have been a reflection of what is in. So, to the extent that the Tree of Life reflects this sense of unity and flow between one world and another, beauty is compassion and compassion beauty. Harmony is at the heart of it all: there is no real separation between selves; we are different voices singing together, different parts of the same music.

Compassion within perseverance. Beauty coupled with endurance.

Hmmm… Sometimes in my journey I become lost, distracted, by the wounds and/or the beauty and power of others. Moving with the grace of *Tiferet sh'b'Netzach,* always toward that which I long for in the biggest, brightest sense, I open to others yet tend to my needs carefully and keep to my path, returning as soon as I know I've strayed. I must worship wisely, with a strong and well-protected heart.

In the spring, I remember the wisdom of winter:

Careful

How do you hold a shard of glass?

Not closely,
not in the palm of your hand.
Your skin isn't meant
for the cradling of sharp things.
Pain and blood will tell you:
do not seek warmth
where only the cold shines!
The arctic glaze, however lovely,
will cut to the bone.
Inhabit your fur
when you travel in unforgiving country.
Bring fire from whatever source.
Worship wisely.
At home in your body,
secure in your breath,
adore the beauty
born in the broken glass.

Bow before every bend of light.

May you be blessed by the beauty within and all
around you, as you journey toward the source of
your beauty. Good night, good morning, good
breathing all.

Bowing to you, O bending lights,
Susan/Shoshana Asiel

Ah, that was a painful relationship, a hard tumble that called forth the wisdom of that poem. A divine thread seemed to pull me through this difficult time, so that I lost myself for only a little while and was able to gather my parts again for the journey that is mine. Thank God for starlight. It's magnetic.

Day 25
Netzach sh'b'Netzach: **Persistence with Persistence**

(Eve of the 25th day, fourth day of the fourth week of the *Omer*.)

bah'Ruch ah'Tah ahdoh'Nai, ehloh'Heynu Meh'lehch ha'oh'Lahm, ah'Shair k'd'Shahnu b'meetz'vo'Tahv, v'tzee'Vahnu Ahl s'fee'Raht hah'O'mer.

> Blessed are You, God, Source of Endurance, You make us holy through Your *mitzvot*, commanding us to count the *Omer*.

ha'Yoam cha'mee'Shah v'ehs'Reem yoam, sh'Heym sh'low'Shah shahvoo'Oat v'ar'bah'Ah ya'Meem lah'O'mer.

> Today is the twenty-fifth day of the *Omer*, which is three weeks and four days of the *Omer*.

Have I told you I am in love with the gate of *Netzach*? And *Netzach sh'b'Netzach* totally dazzles me. Do you have favorite gates? Are there gates that make you glow through and through when you get there?

Continuing, from 2008:

May 14, 2008

Beloved Wanderers—

I spent this morning moving quite consciously through the gate of *Tiferet* within *Netzach*. I set aside my tasks of the week and went to the greening woods to see the May birds. The rose on the breast of the grosbeak, chestnut on the side of the warbler—who could call that mere adornment? It is beauty from within shining out. I went with a friend to share the brilliance of the day. That is compassion, isn't it?—from the Latin "to feel with," to share the experience of feeling. *Tiferet* is both beauty and compassion, brilliance showing from the inside out and beauty shared. Knowing that I was passing through the gate of *Tiferet* within *Netzach*, I decided to trust that all the truly important things of the week, the tasks that move me toward my goals, will get done, perhaps even more efficiently than otherwise, because I am so deliciously nourished and exquisitely well-connected.

Today is the gate of *Netzach* within *Netzach*. The very *Netzach* of *Netzach*—the core of it. "Efficacy' is the word that comes to me for the energy of this gate. We must make ourselves very small, our egos very thin, to get through it. To be truly effective in bringing about the awareness of interdependence that we long for and know is necessary, we cannot be puffed up with importance or intoxicated with our own words. We simply won't make it through the gate. If I have even a glimmer of self-superior or self-diminishing thought, I am stopped in my tracks—I cannot write one word more to you that has any truth in it. Rather than entertain thoughts about myself, positive or negative, I must hearken instead to what glimmers from afar and respond with what answers from within. It takes a certain stepping out of ourselves to enter the wider expanse that is available to us. Commitment to a regular practice of self-thinning helps. *Elecha Yah Ekra.*

Sleepers Awake

Until I take the stars inside
I cannot go back to sleep.
Thank God for porches and decks
for doorknobs and doorways and feet
that step out of my house and into the deep
clarity of night.

Here are two things
two things only to see:
all encompassing darkness and pinholes of
       light—
brilliance, through which, if I had
eyes for it, I could look into
the vastness that holds us.
Failing that, I breathe
and gaze from afar,
make of myself a cup, a small
container of great space: planets and moons
and all that keeps us together
and spinning in our places.

I do not say it is easy
to be both finite and immeasurable—
only that it must be done.

It's the work that makes peace
possible, and waking
a matter of light.

Peace, Wanderers, peace,
Susan/Shoshana Asiel

I suppose we fall in love with what we need. It's one
of God's tricks to help us grow. As I've said before,
I'm basically a *Hod*kind. Present, spontaneous, full of
wow. I move on from one project to the next, leaving
many incomplete and unfinished. I am rather poor at
envisioning outcomes and planning for them. My
study is right now an embarrassing mess, or would be
if I let anyone but my immediate family in it. But there
is in me something that resonates exquisitely with this
gate of persistence and carrying on, eyes on the prize.
As with all lovers, *Netzach* is my teacher. I humbly—
and delightfully—submit. Are you dancing with the
gates, Dear One? Have you fallen in love yet? Don't
forget to enjoy them, as they—of this I am sure—
enjoy you.

Day 26
Hod sh'b'Netzach: **Praise with Persistence**

(Eve of the 26th day, fifth day of the fourth week of the
Omer.)

*bah'Ruch ah'Tah ahdoh'Nai, ehloh'Heynu Meh'lehch
ha'oh'Lahm, ah'Shair k'd'Shahnu b'meetz'vo'Tahv,
v'tzee'Vahnu Ahl s'fee'Raht hah'O'mer.*

> Blessed are You, God, Source of Endurance, You
> make us holy through Your *mitzvot*, commanding us
> to count the *Omer*.

*ha'Yoam shee'Shah v'ehs'Reem yoam, sh'Heym
sh'low'Shah shahvoo'Oat v'cha'mee'Shah ya'Meem
lah'O'mer.*

> Today is the twenty-sixth day of the *Omer*, which is
> three weeks and five days of the *Omer*.

Here comes the gate of my adoration nestled securely
within the gate of my persistence. Powerful medicine
here, for me. I wonder what you will find…

Continuing, from 2008:

> May 15, 2008

> Beloveds—

> Today is twenty-six days, which are three weeks
> and five days, of the *Omer*. We enter today through
> the gate of *Hod* within the gate of *Netzach*. *Hod* is
> an amazing gate; it is associated with humility and
> with glory, with honor and with beauty. Made of
> both a *Hey* (divine revelation) and a *Daled*
> (doorway), it is a gateway of divine breath, of wind
> and spirit, bringing life to earth and filling us with
> the wonder of our earthly being. I love this gate, as I

love the ground beneath my feet and the sky that
makes the ground possible.

Within the gate of Endurance, the gate of Humble
Glory invites us to attend to what is near, what is in
truth all around us, as we walk with confidence
toward what we envision, what we know is calling
us from afar. The Gate of *Hod sh'b'Netzach* is
humble and persistent as moss.

Malkuta

The kingdom of heaven is like the moss
at the foot of a tree
one who lives close to you, unnoticed
unnamed
who cleaves to rock and root
and clings to bark. Luminous
to those who see, the majesty of heaven is
green that will not leave, a soft and simple
          cover
for naked earth.

The canopy of moss gives shelter and shade
to the humble, satisfies the appetite of the
low.
The moss of heaven is like a forest,
magnificent to those who live within.
Catcher of light, holder of holy rain
the majesty of moss is like a chalice set
with shards of sun and pearls of sky.

Treasure beyond measure, precious beyond
          price
the majesty of heaven breathes

at the foot of your tree.

> Breathing deeply at your feet,
> I am
> Susan/Shoshana Asiel

I wrote that poem before I was Jewish. The title, *Malkuta*, is in an Aramaic word, a form of the Hebrew *Malchut*, meaning "royalty," "royal power," or "queenly or kingly dignity." It is the word, according to my Sufi teacher Neil Douglas-Klotz, Jesus would have spoken in his "Kingdom of Heaven" teachings, one of which I will quote here, from the gospel of Matthew, because it is so lovely and earthy, full of *Hod*:[11]

> "The kingdom of heaven is like a grain of mustard seed which a man took and sowed in his field; it is the smallest of all seeds, but when it has grown it is the greatest of all shrubs and becomes a tree, so that the birds of the air come and make nests in its branches." (Mt 13:31)

However you define yourself religiously, Dear One, pay attention to what is small and near; do this with persistence. The forces of distraction are manifold and will throw you off your path. Return then to this simple practice: Ask yourself, "What is here? What is this? Beneath my feet, against my skin, within my chest; what miracle of living am I exploring right now?"

Day 27
Yesod sh'b'Netzach: **Relationship with Persistence**

(Today is the 27th day, sixth day of the fourth week of the *Omer*.)

bah'Ruch ah'Tah ahdoh'Nai, ehloh'Heynu Meh'lehch ha'oh'Lahm, ah'Shair k'd'Shahnu b'meetz'vo'Tahv, v'tzee'Vahnu Ahl s'fee'Raht hah'O'mer.

> Blessed are You, God, Source of Endurance, You make us holy through Your *mitzvot*, commanding us to count the *Omer*.

ha'Yoam shee'Vah v'ehs'Reem yoam, sh'Heym sh'low'Shah shahvoo'Oat v' shee'Shah ya'Meem lah'O'mer.

> Today is the twenty-seventh day of the *Omer*, which is three weeks and six days of the *Omer*.

Dear One, at the gate of *Yesod*, energy gathers and mounts, carrying us into a deeper, more generative place than we have ever been before. So it seems to me. What is your experience as we come around again to this gate of endurance and long-term relationship?

Continuing, from 2008:

May 16, 2008

Beloveds—

Welcome to the gate of *Yesod sh'b'Netzach*, leading us to the very foundation of our strength, to that enduring love which enables us to persist, to carry on. Here is a poem that speaks to me from this gate. It came to me in 1985, as I struggled with what was then my nine-year-old relationship with Wendy, my life partner.

Relationship Poem

for Wendy

Step carefully
when you tread on the earth.
Know every step you take
presses on her body:
her face her forests
brown skin of her mountains
changeable eyes of her lakes.

How easy it is to forget
your long-time lover—
ages it has been
you have shared this bed.
What began in deep reverence
sinks into habit—
your steps grow heavy
you trample
the shoots of love.

Bring your gaze from the stars
to the ground of your being.
She is there beneath you
she is all around you—
she holds you steady
keeps you firm—
do not take for granted
the love in your bones.

How rooted you are
in her love.
She is your home
your strength
your carrying on.
She is the fire
in the core of your heart -
how easy it is to forget
your center.

Twenty-three years, two children, and many shared
meals later, I am glad I listened to the voice that
spoke that poem.

We are born into, and continually through,
relationship. We remember ourselves in one
another. May we do so in good health.

Enduringly yours,
Susan/Shoshana Asiel

This would be a good time, Dear One, to take an
inventory of your daily routines. Whether you live
alone or with others, notice your habits, how you
usually do your mornings, your evenings. Do these

foundational patterns need changing or refreshing? Have you slipped into automatic pilot, so that you do not notice the life you are leading with these habits? How might you add a measure of awareness and appreciation to your days? What shoots of love call out to be noticed as you wend your way to Sinai?

Day 28
Malchut sh'b'Netzach: **Majesty, with Perseverance**

(Eve of the 28th day, seventh day of the fourth week of the *Omer*.)

bah'Ruch ah'Tah ahdoh'Nai, ehloh'Heynu Meh'lehch ha'oh'Lahm, ah'Shair k'd'Shahnu b'meetz'vo'Tahv, v'tzee'Vahnu Ahl s'fee'Raht hah'O'mer.

> Blessed are You, God, Source of Endurance, You make us holy through Your *mitzvot*, commanding us to count the *Omer*.

ha'Yoam sh'moa'Nah v'ehs'Reem yoam, sh'Heym ar'bah'ah shahvoo'Oat lah'O'mer.

> Today is the twenty-eighth day of the *Omer*, which is four weeks of the *Omer*.

Last day of *Netzach*'s week. Have you enjoyed your ride so far? Has it been a little rocky in parts? Have you tumbled from your camel once or twice? It happens. A little extra contact with the earth can be good sometimes. Always, in fact. Yes, always.

Continuing, from 2008:

May 17, 2008

Beloveds—

This is the gate of *Malchut sh'b'Netzach*. Dignity within Perseverance. *Malchut*, the lowest gate in the Tree of Life, lies in the root system: it represents the channels through which our deepest nourishment is carried in support of our highest good. *Malchut* is also our crown. If our roots are deep and strong and the soil we grow in is the kind of soil we need, we will bear ourselves regally in the world, with strength and self-assurance. When we walk with *Malchut*, we move as if we know what we are about. And we do know. We move toward our goals with the bearing of a well-nourished soul. We take our sustenance from the earth beneath our feet, surrendering to that of which we are made. We are moving *b' Malchut Shaddai*—as Rabbi Arthur translates from our liturgy—"with the majesty of nurture." Well nurtured, we exude nurture.

Through the gate of *Malchut*, within the gate of *Netzach*, we remember our prophetic and visionary natures. The truth can come through us easily, when, with *Malchut*, our intention is pure and our foundation strong: opening our mouths, we speak with confidence, or sing full out, the truth of our experience for the good of our communities. With *Netzach's* long view, we understand that we humans are moving, however slowly, toward what we long for—what glimmers from afar, what has always called us and is found deep within and among us:

Moral Values

Don't talk to me about anything but love.
Don't give me religion if it doesn't
shimmer in the waves between us
if it doesn't light
the dungeons that divide
the powerful
from the dispossessed.
It isn't love if it doesn't show us
a way from the pit, give us a hill
to stand on, help us to see
the curve of the world.

Don't give me a ship if it won't
bring us all around safely
to the place
where our journey begins.

November, 2004

Elecha Yah Ekra. To you, I call. To you, I listen.
With you, I begin.

All love always,
Susan/Shoshana Asiel

Well, sometimes the truth comes through me like that, easily and with great assurance. Sometimes I hem and haw. Sometimes, like Jacob, I wrestle my nature to the ground before I begin to grasp it. But this is clear: practice, Dear One, daily practice helps.

Week Five: *Hod*
Splendor, humility, glory of physical forms

Day 29
Chesed sh'b'Hod: **Tenderness within Splendor**

(Eve of the 29th day, the first day of the fifth week of the *Omer*.)

*bah'Ruch ah'Tah ahdoh'Nai, ehloh'Heynu Meh'lehch
ha'oh'Lahm, ah'Shair k'd'Shahnu b'meetz'vo'Tahv,
v'tzee'Vahnu Ahl s'fee'Raht hah'O'mer.*

> Blessed are You, God, Source of Splendor, You
> make us holy through Your *mitzvot*, commanding us
> to count the *Omer*.

*ha'Yoam tee'Shah v'ehs'Reem yoam, sh'Heym ar'bah'Ah
shahvoo'Oat v'Yoam eh'Chod lah'O'mer*

> Today is the twenty-ninth day of the *Omer*, which
> makes four weeks and one day of the *Omer*.

Now we enter the week of *Hod*. Totally at home I am
in this gate. I wrap *Hod* around me like a *tallit*, the
shawl we wear for morning prayers and throughout the
eve and day of *Yom Kippur*, the holiest of holy days,
when all the gates are wide open. Welcome into the
splendor, Dear One. Let's see what we'll find today…

Beloveds,

I am back writing to you in real-time, having returned
yesterday from my travels to Richmond. There, on Sunday,
Hod-in-*Netzach* day, I was in church, leading a service with

poetry and narrative about my journey from Methodism, through Unitarian Universalism, and into Judaism—the expanding circles of my religious identity. It was splendid, truly, to be doing that, there—draped in *tallit* and crowned with *kippah*. As a newly converted Jew who has lived for many years in Philadelphia, in the midst of many knowledgeable and articulate rabbis and Jewish leaders, I am hesitant to consider myself a Jewish teacher. I often feel that I don't know enough. My friends tell me that this is a common feeling among Jewish folk. Our teacher Shefa tells us that being Jewish is not so much about what you know, as about how you practice what you know, and how you explore what you don't know. If I am teaching from the truth of my experience, how could I be wrong or insufficiently informed? I know, for instance, without reading or being told, that wearing a *kippah* reminds me of two things: that I am Jewish and that my head, my thinking self, belongs to more than me. The *tallit* reminds me that I am wrapped in the world and that I take responsibility for the world, from the inside out, and that I share this responsibility with many companions, who also wear the world with reverence. I did not learn these from a book, but from the experience of wearing them, in community. So I taught the children about the *kippah* and *tallit* in the "Message for all Ages" that occurred in the service just before they left for their own classes. In my talk for the grown-ups, I taught the congregation about *tzitzit*, inviting folks to hold and appreciate the sacred threads of their own spiritual journeys, as they listened to me following mine. I called out the *Sh'ma*; some who knew it joined me, each of us holding our threads and listening.

I love to sit on a stone wall. "Look—there's another side to this divide," I call out, "and a gate here, and the gate opens! Come through and explore if you want. You can become Jewish if you like, as I did. Or just come see what treasures can be found across the divide."

I drove home yesterday, robes flowing, crowned all the way, though Wendy warned me on the phone that there was water from a mysterious source on the basement floor of our house. We have had another big drenching after a long, snowy winter and copious spring rains, and there is seepage now from the saturated ground on the other side of our walls—can it be that our dry foundation cannot be called so anymore? Coming through *Yesod* into *Malchut* last night, bringing my glory down to the muddy earth, I found it was time to sop and mop and sweep and bag up what in our basement is no longer necessary to keep. That bin of stuffed animals that no one plays with anymore—we can let them go. Anything that no longer brings joy, goodbye!

Hello to *Hod*, splendor in the mud. Today is *Chesed sh' b'Hod*. Let us love the mud with all our heart and with all our soul and with all our might. Let us find the depth of our caring in the glory of what is. Have I written you of the miners, the West Virginians lost in the Upper Big Branch last week? Have I told you that I come from coal miners, that my people lived and died for generations in the mountains of Wales, and were recruited by the Methodist ministers employed by American mining companies to work in the coal mines of Northeastern Pennsylvania? In the *New York Times* yesterday I saw an image of Barack Obama, his profile thoughtful and somber, standing in front of the rows of 29 simple white crosses at the memorial service for the victims. In his speech, he asked simply and profoundly, "How can we fail them?" Well, we have and we did, but it's a question worth living with, living into, until we change the institutional callousness that allowed their deaths, until we become a culture that makes caring for one another the first thing, a culture that begins with *Chesed*.

Here's a simple thought that surprises me with its force: I am proud of my President. I am proud to have as my leader a thoughtful, brilliant man who cares enough to ask such a question publicly. I am proud of our President, the one we elected. Perhaps I have not said it often or loud enough. There are voices of derision and shame that would silence him, us—they are having a nasty sort of tea party and they must be countered with simple, clear truth. *I am proud of my President.*

The poem that comes to me today to share with you is not one I expected for this gate, but I don't know why I ever bother to expect anything. Better to be continually surprised.

Alligator Medicine

I was borne by the howling wolves,
lifted up to a river in the sky—
there I was cradled in the Milky Way
and delivered
to my home
in the swamp.

I grow strong and swift in the reeds,
give my belly to the oozing earth.
I learn the silence of the sunken log
and the soak
of the sun
in my scales.

I find my jaws a powerful tool—
I use them
when hunger strikes.
I carry my babies in the same toothed cave.
I have always
been female
and fierce.

From what glistens in the mud and in the dark of the caves,

fiercely, tenderly

I am

Yours always,

Shoshana Asiel

Ah, there I am again. *Shoshana Asiel*. No Susan in the
signature. I am enjoying this—growing into my name

through the practice of counting days. But I'll come back to that. I think this is enough for today.

Day 30
Gevurah sh'b' Hod: Strength with Splendor

(Eve of the 30th day, the 2nd day of the fifth week of the *Omer*.)

bah'Ruch ah'Tah ahdoh'Nai, ehloh'Heynu Meh'lehch ha'oh'Lahm, ah'Shair k'd'Shahnu b'meetz'vo'Tahv, v'tzee'Vahnu Ahl s'fee'Raht hah'O'mer.

> Blessed are You, God, Source of Splendor, You make us holy through Your *mitzvot*, commanding us to count the *Omer*.

ha'Yoam sh'low'Sheem yoam, sh'Heym ar'bah'Ah shahvoo'Oat oo'Shnay ya'Meem lah'O'mer.

> Today is the thirtieth day of the *Omer*, which makes four weeks and two days of the *Omer*.

Dear One, reading over yesterday's letter about the miners and my pride in our President, I am saddened to note that I do not, at this moment, feel that pride, or rather the pride I did feel is diluted by repeated disappointments. By the time you read this, the political landscape will have changed again, and I will have a different perspective on my current disappointment, no doubt. So I won't go into what saddens me now. I will instead use the strength of

Gevurah to gather my energy around my personal commitment to justice: how am I called to work right now, and with whom? In what ways am I being invited to reveal the splendor of a truly just way of living? It has not always been clear to me, but I do have a sense of that now. And I am getting about my business. In what ways are you called? What seeds of justice are yours to plant? With whom will you do your planting?

Beloveds,

These gates are having their way with me.

A little over two years ago, just before I finished Shefa's chant leadership training, she and I had a conversation about what I might need to gather and move on as a graduate of the chant leadership training. I tried to slide away quietly:

"Well, I've really enjoyed the whole experience… very nourishing," I told her, "but …well…I'm not very musical and as you know I am not even Jewish." It was perhaps the hundredth time during the course of the eighteenth month training that I had made the 'not-Jewish' assertion. "But why," I wondered out loud to Shefa, "Do I insist on defining myself by what I am not?"

"Good question," Shefa said. "Live with it for a while and see what comes."

I did. I let the question turn in my thoughts, meditations, dreams, notebooks. In the course of that week I remembered an incident in my parents' house as a nineteen-year-old: home on spring break, cooking alone in the family kitchen, I opened the oven door and was met by an awful, disembodied sound, a kind of mad roar, riled human voices perhaps, or perhaps not human at all. I shut the door quickly and forcefully. Later that week, I wrote a poem about the experience, though I changed the word "oven" to "refrigerator." I remember kudos in my poetry writing class for successfully using "refrigerator" in a poem, but other than that nothing remained of the poem or the incident that inspired it—until the aftermath of the conversation with Shefa. The memory of the roar came winging back to me on the letters of the Hebrew word *r'ash*: a word that leapt from the text around the prophet Ezekiel's fiery chariot. In the vision, the word, which can be translated as "roar," "thunder," "earthquake," or "great noise," seems to refer to the thunder of wings. I recognized it as the sound that stunned me from my parents' stove:

R'Ash: The Great Roar

> *for Shefa Gold and every*
> *living Jew*

Fifty-six years. It's time.
I've been shuffling, shifting,
running away
for more generations than I can count.

I closed a door in my heart
because of a roar I heard
from my parents' stove—
I was nineteen, standing alone
by the oven's mouth.

Now I hear through that opened door
the long roar of my own wanderings,
distant thunder,
early rumblings of a great love
returning—
an unspeakable power
searching for itself
in me?
Two thousand years and more:
I come home now
to the miracle of you
standing here,
alive, golden,
calling to me
through the murderous times

Kadosh, Kadosh, Kadosh
Holy, Holy, Holy

And the quaking
beneath my feet
and in my knees?
It's what happens to the earth
when the truth breaks through—
I am ready for the fire:

one God, one People, one Earth
one impeccable Voice.

I want that power
in this world.

January 29, 2008

There was my answer to the question, "Why am I defining myself by what I am not?" Not so much an answer as a commandment: *Do this: Become Jewish.* Perhaps the fear of the great roar was the reason I seemed to be using only half of my voice—speaking well enough, but not fully singing, holding back from exploring the full range of tones available to me. I am Jewish now, several years into it, and using much more of the voice that is available to me, in song, in speech, in living out my life. And there are many of you now to help me understand, to steady me when I tremble and to help me let the power, the strength, the *Gevurah* of the Universe, find itself through me.

It is a Great Love indeed that searches with such vigor.

All praises to that Love.

Shoshana Asiel

Whew. Some messages come through with such strength and clarity, we just can't miss them. Other messages try to come through, but we're not ready, as was the case with my nineteen-year-old self. I was barely becoming Susan then. It was not time for me to know *Shoshana Asiel*, this lily-made-of-Godstuff—I had not yet found the supports that could help me with this opening. Our stories unfold in time. That's the way of humans. So I give a reverent nod to the Infinite, a yes to the here and now, and a bow to the perfect timing of it all.

I wonder about the story of your names, Dear One. How have you been called? How are you called now? How do you want to be called? How do you feel in your names? Perhaps in the week of splendor, you'll want to spend some time with the sound, the meaning, the vibration, the splendor of your name, or your names, just as they are now. Appreciate, enjoy, be curious and open to change, the right change for the right time. No other changes are necessary. So speaks the gate of *Gevurah sh'b'Hod*.

Day 31
Tiferet sh'b' Hod: The Beauty of Praise

(Eve of the 31st day, the third day of the fifth week of the *Omer*.)

bah'Ruch ah'Tah ahdoh'Nai, ehloh'Heynu Meh'lehch ha'oh'Lahm, ah'Shair k'd'Shahnu b'meetz'vo'Tahv, v'tzee'Vahnu Ahl s'fee'Raht hah'O'mer.

> Blessed are You, God, Source of Splendor, You make us holy through Your *mitzvot*, commanding us to count the *Omer*.

ha'Yoam eh'chod oo'sh'low'Sheem yoam, sh'Heym
ar'bah'Ah shahvoo'Oat oo'sh'low'Shah ya'Meem
lah'O'mer.

Today is the thirty-first day of the *Omer*, which
makes four weeks and three days of the *Omer*.

Tiferet again. Prepare to open your wings.

Beloveds,

The beauty of praise is that we don't know why we do it.
But somehow when we raise our voices to express an
overwhelming sense of gratitude for our being, we
understand that this is what we are born for, to open our
mouths and sing to the very breath of life, though it makes
no sense at all.

Sh'ma

What is this smile, this slight
pause, this tipped-back comma
in my chest? A miniscule thing
easily ignored, yet growing
larger for being looked at, into—
larger yet for being felt.

The space a question makes around a thing
a true question, not closed at the end
a knotted loop to catch or kill
but open, cupped like an ear—
that's what I want to offer

that's what I want to wrap around
every mystery, every gleaming
crescent of moon in the bone of my breast.

What is this moon, this shining
yellow bowl in the deepening blue:
leaning against the edge of day?
What is this blue
that holds me as I rise, this
robe of indigo that clothes me every night
this night that wakes me with its piercing
       lights?
What is this me, shot through with joy?
What is this joy, this sweet,

unspeakable sound?

Today I enjoy the broadening energy of *Tiferet* within the humble glory of *Hod*. I lean into my questions and listen. I do not need answers. Singing, with a smile that is not entirely my own, is more than enough. What am I singing today? What I've been singing all week: *K'doshim ti'h'Yu ki kaDosh Ani* (Lev. 19:2): You shall be holy, for I am holy.[12] That's all there is to it: we are holy, you and I. There is this central happiness in the heart of us. Do you sense it? If you don't, or if you feel a smidge of holiness and would like to expand it, try chanting or simply breathing with the words *K'doSheem ti'h'Yu kee kaDosh Ani*... until you do. Then commit to living from that place.

Much love,

Shoshana Asiel

I think I'll leave you today with the above practice,
Dear One. If the Hebrew is unfamiliar to you, chant or
breathe in the English: You are holy for I am holy.
That's the truth. Take it from a lily.

Day 32
Netzach sh'b' Hod: The Persistence of Glory

(Eve of the 32nd day, the fourth day of the fifth week of the
Omer.)

*bah'Ruch ah'Tah ahdoh'Nai, ehloh'Heynu Meh'lehch
ha'oh'Lahm, ah'Shair k'd'Shahnu b'meetz'vo'Tahv,
v'tzee'Vahnu Ahl s'fee'Raht hah'O'mer.*

> Blessed are You, God, Source of Splendor, You
> make us holy through Your *mitzvot*, commanding us
> to count the *Omer*.

*ha'Yoam sh'Nai'eem v'sh'low'Sheem yoam, sh'Heym
ar'bah'Ah shahvoo'Oat v'ar'bah'Ah ya'Meem lah'O'mer.*

> Today is the thirty-second day of the *Omer*, which
> makes four weeks and four days of the *Omer*.

Netzach in *Hod*. The light that glimmers from afar,
Dear One, glimmers also in the dust of which we are
made. The radiance of these gates is powerful,
persistently so. It knocks me over sometimes.

Beloveds,

I am inclined to go into a kind of depression after a major opening. There is a part of me that wants to keep myself from changing too fast. That's a positive spin on the sluggishness that sometimes overcomes me, and it can be a useful way to work with the energy of depression—to use it as a message to slow down a bit, take stock, self-nurture, pray more, chant more, dance more. But when depression begins to dig in, it keeps me from growing at all. Perhaps my depressive episodes try to save me from death by keeping me in the same place, freezing me where I am, as if paralysis will keep me alive, as if not-growing will keep my death away.

I love the way *Netzach* reminds me to chip away at my petrified energy—to be persistent in my practices. There is a world of light, I learn, that can be found, with practice, inside the stone of my frightened self. There will be time enough to be stone, I hear, when I listen. I know from the whispers of the rocks I live among, the Pre-Cambrian quartzite and the schist of my beloved Wissahickon Valley, that being a rock is a wondrous thing. Think of all we get to witness as stone! But now is the time to breathe, and to keep on breathing.

My Rising

Every morning I rise to meet you.
Every day is a decision
to join or not to join
in the turning of the earth.
It is a matter of choice, this dance:
to stand again and step away
from the familiar worries of a private bed
into the waking world.
Some days it's all I have to offer:
the bare minimum: a basic willingness
to turn, face the morning sky and
let myself be—whirled
one more time.

You say it's no small thing,
my rising. You whisper, hum,
begin even to sing
of gratefulness: how my clouded face
shows up for centuries
in your window every day.
The lids of my eyes, half-shut,
half-open, are a field,
a place on which to drop
seeds that fall like kisses or
kisses that fall like seeds.

You say my offering is savory to you
and sweet.
The sacrifice you want is a simple one.

I say: but this living is
more terrible than I want to know.

I offer you this day an unbearable heaviness:
weight of the curtain
dropped on my sister's eyes.
I say: I am counting corpses of children
and bullets that tear my city's streets,
confess
I have not done enough to stop them.
Nor have I done enough, I fear,
to protect and prepare my own sons.

You say: *enough, enough.*
You are fed, satisfied, pleasured even
by my daily risings.
The bread I give you is my breath
wandering out to find you
as I am, as you are, as we
have always been.

A new world is coming in these mornings—
do you see?

Oh my dearest companions, may these writings find you persistently, sweetly breathing.

B'shalom,

Susan/Shoshana Asiel

There is Susan again. I guess I'll never quite leave her behind. Not in this life at any rate. And if I do, for a time, I must go back and pick her up again. She does slow me down some; she can be heavy baggage with her worries and her cowering. But it is not a bad thing to move slowly. It is possible to take in more of what surrounds us when we amble rather than run. When my aging mother's walk began to slow down to what seemed to me an insufferable pace, I was often impatient, and I barely disguised it. I regret that restlessness. I think of the moments I missed with her by not being fully present in what was real. Take a slow walk today, Dear One; appreciate yourself and the ones around you as you are this very day. Notice what glimmers from the dust that is near.

Day 33
Hod sh'b'Hod: Glory within Glory

(Eve of the 33rd day, the fifth day of the fifth week of the *Omer*.)

bah'Ruch ah'Tah ahdoh'Nai, ehloh'Heynu Meh'lehch ha'oh'Lahm, ah'Shair k'd'Shahnu b'meetz'vo'Tahv, v'tzee'Vahnu Ahl s'fee'Raht hah'O'mer.

> Blessed are You, God, Source of Splendor, You make us holy through Your *mitzvot*, commanding us to count the *Omer*.

ha'Yoam sh'low'Shah oo'sh'low'Sheem yoam, sh'Heym ar'bah'Ah shahvoo'Oat v'cha'mee'Shah ya'Meem lah'O'mer.

> Today is the thirty-third day of the *Omer*, which makes four weeks and four days of the *Omer*.

This is a new day, Dear One. Are you grateful that you are here, now? Are you curious what will come to you today—what the enveloping night will offer in the way of whispers and dreams and what surprises the amazing daylight will bring? Are you open? Expectant? Present and willing, at least? This is all that is required.

Beloveds,

This is a special day, a festival day—*Lag b'Omer*, the thirty-third day, fifth day of the fifth week of the *Omer*— it's a good day for a haircut, a wedding, a walk in the woods, especially with bows and arrows and a *Torah* scroll hidden in your pack.[13] There are many legends associated with this day, but why we celebrate it remains a bit mysterious. Maybe it's just something about May that calls out for a celebration, for shooting at demons, dancing with trees. Or maybe it's the *sefirot* themselves calling us—a double portion of *Hod* on this day: glory within glory, humility within humility, earthiness of the earth itself, the holy play of creation. Take an extra *Shabbat* today if you can, or at least find some new way to play. Have some deep fun.

I wrote this poem when I left the Methodist church for the Unitarian Universalist one in our neighborhood. At that time we were a bi-religious family, and our second son, the baptized child of my womb, made the switch with me.

Psalm

When I tried to explain
to my six-year-old son Gregory
what a Unitarian is
he said I don't think it matters
what religion you are
what matter is
are you fun to play with?
I said yeah
and how we treat each other
that's important, isn't it?
He said Mhmm…
Are you fun to play with?
I thought about how tired I get
some evenings
when it's our time together
and I can barely drag up enough energy
to read a book
and all the while I'm thinking about
the phone calls I need to make
come eight-thirty—
Are you fun to play with?
Sometimes before bed he tells me
he's afraid of fire
and spends all his time being scared
our house will burn down.
I tell him we have good neighbors
who would take us in—
he says he hopes we go next door
to live with Nate
because he's fun to play with.
And if we have to move away
because of the fire

can we take our neighbors with us?
Are you fun to play with?
And you know what else? he says
when I'm having fun
I don't think about any of these things.

And now I'm thinking about that God
in Psalm 104
the one some, not all, Unitarians believe in
the one who covers herself with light
as with a garment
and stretches out the heavens
like a tent
who makes the winds
his messengers
and fire and flame
her helping hands.
I'm thinking how the waters
once stood
above the mountains
how the mountains rose
and the valleys sank down
and springs now flow
between the hills.
Are you fun to play with?
Look!
There's the sea, the Psalmist says,
teeming with creatures
great and small!
There go the ships—
and there!
diving to the deep
and leaping for the wide
blue sky

go the humpback whales—

Are you fun to play with?

Are you?

That's it for today, sweet ones. Enjoy!

Susan/Shoshana Asiel

May the blessings of *Lag b'Omer* upon you, Dear One.
Double *Hod* to you!

Day 34
Yesod sh'b'Hod: The Foundation of Glory

(Eve of the 34th day, the sixth day of the fifth week of the
Omer.)

*bah'Ruch ah'Tah ahdoh'Nai, ehloh'Heynu Meh'lehch
ha'oh'Lahm, ah'Shair k'd'Shahnu b'meetz'vo'Tahv,
v'tzee'Vahnu Ahl s'fee'Raht hah'O'mer.*

> Blessed are You, God, Source of Splendor, You
> make us holy through Your *mitzvot*, commanding us
> to count the *Omer*.

*ha'Yoam ar'bah'Ah oo'sh'low'Sheem yoam, sh'Heym
ar'bah'Ah shahvoo'Oat v' shee'Shah ya'Meem lah'O'mer.*

> Today is the thirty-fourth day of the *Omer*, which
> makes four weeks and six days of the *Omer*.

Did you find some fun yesterday, some way to revel in the glory of the growing sun? I hope so. If you forgot, well, there's always another chance for joy. Welcome to this new beginning.

Beloveds,

The foundation of glory is love, that which binds us one to another, to our lives, and to the places where we live our lives.

This Place

Every so often in the course of seasons
comes a time when you know once again
the place you have chosen to be
is the place that has chosen you.

It's like that now in azalea time
when the face of nearly every stone house
blossoms forth in all manner of pink.
Soft purple and salmon spill

over and down the slopes of yards,
making the very pavement ache.
Cars slow down to listen
to the rolling mezzo
tones of red, and to savor
the smell of earth and sweat
in the thickness of petals.

Every so often comes a time

when you meet the face of your desire
and you choose
to let yourself be wanted.

Sometimes it's like that— the day is graced with
extraordinary bliss and the deepest understandings. Other
days, this one for instance, are full of annoying encounters,
even though I live, as now, in the midst of full open azaleas
and the most magnificent drape of deepening green.
Yesterday I told you to take an extra *Shabbat* if you could.
For me, though, this was a working Sunday; I was co-
teaching a poetry workshop in a synagogue with which I
was unacquainted for a large group of third through sixth
grades I had never taught before. My co-teacher called me
an hour before the workshop to say she could not make it—
did she want me to talk through her parts of the teaching? I
was annoyed that she hadn't given me an earlier heads up
instead of waiting until the moment I needed to be leaving
my house. Then, after teaching the class, I was annoyed
with myself for not being at the top of my game. On the
way home, I went to my food co-op to pick up what we
needed for dinner but found, at the cash register, my
pocketbook empty of wallet. I was extremely annoyed with
myself for leaving it in the pack I had taken to the woods
yesterday for Wendy's and my *Shabbat* walk. Although I
was relieved that the wallet hadn't been lost or stolen at the
synagogue, I was still annoyed with myself for being so
annoyed on *Lag b'Omer* when I should have been basking
in the humble glory of praise.

Within the framework of the forty-nine gates, particularly this week of *Hod*, I come to understand that annoyance is a form of arrogance. Vanity is the underside of *Hod*, the curious underbelly of honor, and what is arrogance but the bloat of vanity? What am I saying of myself when I feel "annoyed"? That I am somehow too good for this, that whatever the irritation is, I do not deserve it, that I should be having a better day than the one I am having? Sometimes I am even too good for myself. Don't I deserve better than this forgetful, distracted, easily flapped thing that I am?

I went home to retrieve myself, the little packet of identity I had carelessly misplaced, so that I could return to my co-op and claim the bag of groceries the cashier had kindly put in the walk-in refrigerator for me. And because it was *Lag b'Omer*, I decided to slow down a bit, to take the time to have lunch before setting out on the rest of my errands. Then I decided, because it was *Lag b'Omer*, that perhaps I could manage to enjoy the things I had to do: buying a bottle of wine for dinner, picking up new ink cartridges for my printer, redeeming my bag of groceries. A chant would be helpful, a few words of *Torah*, could perhaps assist. So I replaced my inner complaints with this: *K'doShim ti'h'Yu ki kaDosh Ani.* "You shall be holy, for I am holy." Much better. With my afternoon errands threaded thus together in the remembrance of holiness, each encounter on my route was pleasant and sweet.

So I am taking up a new spiritual practice. I've decided to drop the word "annoying" from my vocabulary and to chant the holiness of all every time the feeling of annoyance sweeps in. This was how I celebrated *Lag b'Omer* today. It's been a humble kind of fun.

And the gate we turn to—*Yesod sh'b' Hod*? I think the key to this gate is in the poem I began with. So many complaints have filled up the pages since I began this missive that you might want to take a moment and read the poem again. A poem, like a chant, gives amply to the one who returns to it.

This is a day to honor the passion we have for being here, wherever "here" is; it is a day to let ourselves be wanted, drawn, by the splendor of the world as it is and the even greater splendor of the worlds within the world we see, the secret voices, the quiet humming. Make a life out of that— listen to that, love that, commit everything to that. Let every distraction bring you home.

Have I told you that you, too, are the faces of my desire? I have chosen to let you happen to me, to let myself breathe here with you, in you, through you. I will get distracted. You can count on it. But count also on my return.

Thank you for being here.

All love and honor,
Susan/Shoshana Asiel

Are you able to take in this love and honor, Dear One? Can you sense how I revere you for being here, on day 34, still? Or for having returned, if you've been away? I bow to your commitment.

Day 35
Malchut sh'b'Hod: **Surrender in Praise**

(Eve of the 35th day, the seventh day of the fifth week of the *Omer*.)

bah'Ruch ah'Tah ahdoh'Nai, ehloh'Heynu Meh'lehch ha'oh'Lahm, ah'Shair k'd'Shahnu b'meetz'vo'Tahv, v'tzee'Vahnu Ahl s'fee'Raht hah'O'mer.

> Blessed are You, God, Source of Splendor, You make us Holy through Your *mitzvot*, commanding us to count the *Omer*.

ha'Yoam chah'mee'Shah oo'sh'low'Sheem yoam, sh'Heym chah'mee'Shah shahvoo'Oat lah'O'mer.

> Today is the thirty-fifth day of the *Omer*, which makes five weeks of the *Omer*.

Get ready to give it up, Dear One. Whatever it is you may be holding on to, or holding back from—this is a good day to begin the letting go.

Beloveds,

I don't know what to say. I just want to sink down where I
am and dissolve in praise of the earth. It is unseasonably
hot and sticky. The air, uncharacteristic for this time of the
year, zings and zaps with mosquitoes. But I have given up
annoyance, so all is well. A rose-breasted grosbeak,
traveling north for the spring, perched on our sunflower
seed feeder this morning. I stood at the screen in my
kitchen doorway for at least ten divine minutes, completely
dazzled as the bird picked seed after seed from the cylinder,
the full fuchsia of his breast fully displayed against a
gleaming white belly. Then later, after accomplishing what
on another day this introvert might have called an annoying
task—soliciting donations from local restaurants for a
community arts organization fundraiser—I was rewarded
by two male orioles, inky black and flame orange. They
were fluttering among the branches of a nearby maple tree,
engaged in the most intimate and energetic conversation—
two stunning males apparently enjoying each other's
company. At least that's what it looked like to me. Lovely
to see and hear!

So I go to this poem, remembering another dazzling
moment from another time.

In the Garden State

At twenty-one, traveling through
the unbearable blue of a June evening, fresh

from Pomp and Circumstance, a passenger
in the front seat of my father's car,
on the familiar route south
over the twin bridges of the Amboys
past the exits of every tightly budgeted
family trip:
Sandy Hook, Asbury Park, Seaside Heights

looking inland
away from Tilt-a-Whirls
and crowded sands, taffy and forgotten halls,
toward the sun, scarlet orb
hung low over the wetlands
pouring over the brilliant grasses,
I was stirred, in parts unspoken,
by the fingers of a cerulean tide,
and flung my turned head back
to gape, gawk, glisten
as long as I wanted.

I saw no shame anywhere
under the shedding light,
heard only *paradise*, only
the garden
and knew it was

my home.

I write during what is not yet the aftermath of the Great
Gulf Drilling Disaster—or whatever it will be called in the
history books—as the spewing oil rises, moves massively
toward the coast, soon to land, if it hasn't already.

We couldn't do what we do to our shores—we wouldn't take such chances with them— if we knew how to properly adore them, remembering that we are here to praise. We would have to find other means to fuel ourselves than digging deeper and deeper into the ocean floor for what doesn't belong to us. Perhaps we would have to do with less and share more as we search for better ways of living together. I try to breathe deeply and expansively around the ache that gathers inside me. I pray that the learning we receive from this horror will turn our heads in the right direction once and for all, for good.

I do not know how long it will take. I bow and ask to receive from the earth the wisdom I need to do the work I can for her, for us. Teach me, I say, how best to love you.

Blessings on us all,
Shoshana Asiel/Lily, Made of God

I'm tired of holding back, tired of being less than myself, tired of covering the essence of my nature— this ecstatic, God-constructed lily that I know myself to be, the one who knows how to praise, how to adore, how to play my part beautifully in the unfolding story of justice. I am dropping the old embarrassments. *Hineni*, Dear One. I'm here.

Week Six: *Yesod*
Intimacy, foundation, long-lasting relationship

Day 36
Chesed sh'b'Yesod: **Love with Commitment**

(Eve of the 36th day, the first day of the sixth week of the *Omer*.)

bah'Ruch ah'Tah ahdoh'Nai, ehloh'Heynu Meh'lehch ha'oh'Lahm, ah'Shair k'd'Shahnu b'meetz'vo'Tahv, v'tzee'Vahnu Ahl s'fee'Raht hah'O'mer.

> Blessed are You, God, Source of All Our Bonds, You make us holy through Your *mitzvot*, commanding us to count the *Omer*.

Ha Yoam shee'Shah oo'sh'low'Sheem Yoam, sh'Heym chah'mee'Shah sha'voo'Oat v'Yoam eh'Chod lah O'mer.

> Today is the thirty-sixth day of the *Omer*, which is five weeks and one day of the *Omer*.

Hello there. We begin a new week; we open a new gate. I notice in myself a sensation of energy powerfully gathered and powerfully gathering, and I notice at once a familiar resistance, a kind of, "Oh no must I start again? Will it hurt?" This is natural enough, I suppose. There is necessary friction in the growing process. A very wise woman I know once taught me that irritation is the beginning of creativity. You may notice it now and again in yourself. How are you this day, Dear One?

Beloveds,

I didn't sleep much last night. The rose triangle on the breast of the grosbeak kept waking me. It is a shape that tapers from the shoulders to a fine point, shimmering down the bird's white belly in a column of fuchsia not unlike what I have seen on the belly of the Atlantic Ocean, as the rose gold ball of sun lifts from the horizon on a clear morning. How to sleep with such beauty continually forming within and all around me? Writing to you is a gorgeous thing—sometimes I think I will burst with the splendor of what is possible between us.

Today, thankfully, begins the week of *Yesod*—foundation, commitment, bonding, long-term relationship, a strong container for the divine flow. *Yesod* is the channel, a trunk for the river of light that passes between the roots above and the roots below. *Yesod* begins with the sound of our English letter '*y*', sound of the Hebrew *yud* ('), the tiny stroke that hangs above the other letters and is the first letter of the unpronounceable Name of God. This little stroke begins many of our prophets' and biblical leaders' names: *Yitz'chak, Ya'akov, Yisrael, Yehoshua, Yoel, Yoneh, Yeheskiel, Yeheshaya, Yirmiyahu*, and, I might add, *Yeshua*, as well as the name of the City of Peace for which we long, *Yerushalayim*. It is the first sound of our English "Yes." Yes, I will let these truths pass through me. Yes, I will open to them, day after day.

I must actively and willfully renew this commitment daily because there are times, like now, when I am tired from a poor night's sleep and do not think I can do it—open again. At these times, it is the commitment that carries me. I have lived in partnership with one woman for thirty-four years. Commitment goes a long way in matters of love—I know this.

Chesed sh'b'Yesod. I keep this commitment to love and to express my love. I do it even when I think I can't or don't particularly want to. This is the kind of thing I tell my students about writing poetry when they feel they have nothing to say: just write it—begin with can't if that's what feels true. Be kind to the part of you that says 'I can't'— give it some space on the page. The words you need will come as you write them."

A Word

A word is a way to know you.
A word is a door, an opening,
window to the world.

A word is a key. You can use it
to unlock things that trouble.
Let the breeze of a word refresh
a room closed up for years.

Almost any word, spoken with love, can do
            this.
But let the words work together, and ah!

that's when a meadow happens.
There are no doors, no windows, no rooms,
    no houses.
There is only us: the wind-swept earth, the
    ground
from which every spring rises.

Sheridan Elementary School,
2007

Grateful to be us.

Wish me a good night's sleep tonight.

Loving you,
Susan/Shoshana Asiel

And you, Dear One, may you be nourished by the milk of kindness in your sleep, in the many hours of your waking, and in all the spaces between. This is how we grow.

Day 37
Gevurah sh' b'Yesod: **Strength within Commitment**

(Eve of the 37th day, the second day of the sixth week of the *Omer*.)

bah'Ruch ah'Tah ahdoh'Nai, ehloh'Heynu Meh'lehch ha'oh'Lahm, ah'Shair k'd'Shahnu b'meetz'vo'Tahv, v'tzee'Vahnu Ahl s'fee'Raht hah'O'mer.

Blessed are You, God, Source of All Our Bonds,
You make us holy through Your *mitzvot*,
commanding us to count the *Omer*.

Ha Yoam shee'Vah oo'sh'low'Sheem Yoam, sh'Heym
chah'mee'Shah sha'voo'Oat oo'Shnay ya'Meem lah'Omer.

Today is the thirty-seventh day of the *Omer*, which
is five weeks and two days of the *Omer*.

Good day to you, Dear One, or good evening.
Whenever this message finds you in your day, may
you be strengthened and firmed, so that you will
properly contain and channel the flow that is your life.

Beloveds,

V'nahar yotzei me'eden, l'hashkot et haGan. A river flows
from Eden to water the garden (Gen. 2:10).[14] This is my
chant for the week of *Yesod*. *Yesod* is a firm, bonding kind
of energy, and *Gevurah* also has a certain grip to it. I want
to make sure there is something delightful and nourishing
running through them. Sometimes I hold myself so tightly
that nothing much can get through, a temptation to control
rather than contain and channel the abundance, the
overflow of energy that is the truth of my being.

I did have a decent night's sleep last night—thank you for
your good wishes. I woke just a little earlier than I might
have chosen with the above words from Genesis on my
lips, knowing that they were the words with which I would

begin my writing to you. And there's another Hebrew word that I love, also from Genesis: *b'ray'Sheet*. From Neil Douglas-Klotz, I learned that it can be translated also as "in the beginning-ness," or even "before the first beginning." The word itself is a celebration of the creative process, which begins always before the beginning. Ah, but how good it is to know the beginning of something, to feel the beginning-ness begin to happen. Then the words flow as from a secret stream. This was a good way for me to wake this morning, and I thank you.

Gevurah and *Yesod* are sturdy gates. Within them, I need not be frightened of what comes through. There are banks to the river and a bonding energy as of the rocks and stones that change ever so slowly, over time. The rocks dally with the stream, hold the water for a while, and let it go— ecstatic dances! Sometimes, when the force is strong, the banks of the stream are carved out, widened. That is the way of soil and water, a different kind of dance. But my banks are strong today, and the flow steady, yet full.

Here's a poem I wrote seven or eight years ago during what was for me a stormy time.

Human

Do not be frightened when beauty strikes
though it leaves you mute and sleepless
churning and roiling like a sea
struck by some sudden turn of wind.
It is only the sun that does this—

the source of light plays
through the atmosphere and changes
everything it touches, always.

If this is happening to you in a violent way
threatening your very core
if beauty feels more blade than blessing
your life more blood than stone
be glad in your grief you are human
grateful for the liquid in your pith—lean

into the beauty that never leaves you
the only life that truly lights you.

I did lean then, and I do lean now, with the difference that now I am more thoroughly supported. *Mah tovu ohalecha Yakov. Mishkanotecha Y'srael*: How good are your tents, Jacob, your dwelling places, Oh God-wrestler, Oh human one (Num. 24: 5). And very good too are these double gates.

I do need a good heart-rending sob, though, or perhaps a roar, about the oil in the waters of the Gulf of Mexico. It is coming.

Today, by the way, is the third full day that the grosbeak, fuchsia-breasted, has come to the feeder in our backyard. Maybe not just passing through? Maybe taking up residence? Most likely not, but I can't help hoping. I'll keep you posted.

Yours ever,

Susan/Shoshana Asiel

It is a good day to consider, re-consider, the practices
that support you, Dear One. How are you doing at
maintaining the sacred container of Self? Who or what
might you enlist to help you? Which are the
relationships that support the growth of your soul?
Make a commitment to find, build, and strengthen
these.

Day 38
Tiferet sh'b'Yesod: Beauty with Commitment

(Eve of the 38th day, the third day of the sixth week of the
Omer.)

*bah'Ruch ah'Tah ahdoh'Nai, ehloh'Heynu Meh'lehch
ha'oh'Lahm, ah'Shair k'd'Shahnu b'meetz'vo'Tahv,
v'tzee'Vahnu Ahl s'fee'Raht hah'O'mer.*

> Blessed are You, God, Source of All Our Bonds,
> You make us holy through Your *mitzvot*,
> commanding us to count the *Omer*.

*Ha Yoam sh'mo'Nah oo'sh'low'Sheem Yoam, sh'Heym
chah'mee'Shah shah'voo'Oat oo'sh'low'Sheem ya'Meem
lah'Omer.*

> Today is the thirty-eighth day of the *Omer*, which is
> five weeks and three days of the *Omer*.

Have you examined your commitment to beauty lately, Dear One? It would be in the spirit of the day to do so...

Beloveds,

I wrote this poem some years ago for my sister. I say it to you now from the gates of *Tiferet* in *Yesod*, which is a day to revivify our bonds, to renew the heart of our relationships, to experience the beauty between us and to celebrate the harmonies we can make when our souls are singing.

From the St. Lawrence River

I wanted to bring you
something from this island:
a rock to stand on,
some rare and ancient fern.
A river of sunlight,
basket of birch bark,
white pines rising
from pink granite,
the shape of the wind.
I wanted to bring you
something you can count on:
a thousand useless islands
broken and worn,
stitched like shards of jade
into the dazzling blue
robe of the river.

It's a robe for you to wear, *tallit* for your morning prayers. I want you to have it because my heart tells me that the text of the natural world is the text that will save us all, is saving us now when we listen, explore, and praise to our hearts' content. Yesterday I spoke with Shefa, who is all about praise these days. She said that the ancient text of *Pirak Shira* (Songs of Praise) that she is studying now is useful insofar as it points to the text of the earth as the real subject to be "studied." And to study means so much more than to observe, or simply to think about, doesn't it? We must climb inside a text, so that we feel the light of the letters, as well as their darkness, next to our skin. Then we may find out what to say, how to live.

Are you wearing your robes, dear and precious earthlings? Are you singing your songs? Are you dazzling everyone you meet with the blue that never ends, the green that ever grows? If we call out in love and awe from the depths of our hearts, we will in time spread the river of sunlight over all. It will happen that way, naturally. I know this.

Having said that, let me also say that I get a little bit scared traversing these three gates, *Chesed, Gevurah*, and the great integrator of the heart, *Tiferet*. Perhaps I have already told you this? Well, perhaps so, but repetition of important truths never hurts, so know that here I am again, afraid that maybe I won't make it through this time. Maybe I should run back or make myself so small that no great power could ever find me, or close up a bit so nothing too large could possibly get through. There are words from the morning liturgy that help. Shefa has a chant for them: *"V'yachayd l'vavaynu l'ahavah u'l'yirah et sh'mecha.* Unify our hearts to love and be in awe of your name/essence."[15]

I sit in the garden and chant this text. My eyes are open, and I see that I'm draped in leaves, fresh and fragrant.

It seems that the grosbeaks (there were two males—did I tell you?) have moved on, but they leave behind an indelible trail of fuchsia. I am happy to have been so marked.

All love,

Susan/Shoshana Asiel

And you too, Dear One, are marked by the trail of fuchsia and the dazzling robe of rivers. How do you bear your beauty in this world? How do you wear your colors? We humans are given the difficult gift of self-consciousness, which we must learn and then unlearn when it no longer serves us; we must turn our self-consciousness into something broader and deeper, which we might call self-awareness, or just awareness— awareness of self, awareness of other.

In your meditation today, Beautiful One, here is something you might try: locate and practice your shimmer: close your eyes, breathe gently into your heart space, and let go into the simple act of listening for a while. Take fifteen or twenty minutes, perhaps.

Listen inside. Listen outside. Notice every vibration of the world around you and the world within. Enjoy the particular resonance that is you. You may hum or sing if you want to, or simply sit in harmonious silence. What colors or combinations of colors come to mind in the silence? Take note. As you enjoy the uniqueness of your shimmer, you may find yourself asking, if you are ready to ask, "What more shall I do with this abundance of light? How may my beauty serve?" When the answers begin to come, be prepared to commit.

Day 39
Netzach sh'b' Yesod: Persistence within Commitment

(Eve of the 39th day, the fourth day of the sixth week of the *Omer*.)

bah'Ruch ah'Tah ahdoh'Nai, ehloh'Heynu Meh'lehch ha'oh'Lahm, ah'Shair k'd'Shahnu b'meetz'vo'Tahv, v'tzee'Vahnu Ahl s'fee'Raht hah'O'mer.

> Blessed are You, God, Source of All Our Bonds, You make us holy through Your *mitzvot*, commanding us to count the *Omer*.

Ha Yoam tee'Shah oo'sh'low'Sheem Yoam, sh'Heym chah'mee'Shah shah'voo'Oat v'ar'bah'Ah ya'Meem lah'Omer.

> Today is the thirty-ninth day of the *Omer*, which is five weeks and four days of the *Omer*.

Did you practice your shimmer yesterday? Or perhaps today? I am curious how that goes for you.

Beloveds,

Here is today's poem. I picked it last year for this gate. Let's see what it brings us.

Spring of my Spring

He's back again, the little bird
with a drill of a song.
See how he cleaves to the branch
by the hanging box that swings
so hopefully in the Rose of Sharon.
He is all song, every brown inch.
Again, again, he insists,
I want this all again!
Tremulous fistful of life
like our first born Gabriel,
intense, insistent messenger,
wanting everything he loved over and over
again and again.

Thank you, persistent one,
for needing me. Thank you
spring of my spring, for reminding me
that an empty house
aches to be thoroughly
inhabited, wholly
lived in, to rock with appetite,
bulge with voice, and fledge out fully
into summer mornings.

Again, again,
tell me the story again,

O little wren, holy one.

They are at it again, the house wrens in the Rose of Sharon.
They are so close to our kitchen, fluttering about one of
several real estate choices we have put out for them in our
yard. And I am once again drawn in by their drama. I think
they are moving in. I hope so. The male's long, insistent,
repetition of song, which I could imagine to some might be
annoying, brings me endless delight.

What do I love so about *Netzach*? Whenever I come around
again to this gate, I am in some important way home to
myself. *Netzach* is the first big gate I shepherded back in
2008, when I wasn't officially Jewish yet, though I knew I
was headed there—here, I mean. Within the gate of
Netzach, I rest again in my ability to persevere as I
remember that what I am moving perpetually towards is my
heart's desire. The light that glimmers from afar resonates
in the rhythm of my pulse. To find *Netzach* within *Yesod* is
a powerful thing—a big YES, again, here. I'll do it. I'll
carry on! For the generations to come, I will give what I
have to give.

It's so simple and clear what we've got to do, in spite of the
great, monstrous glob of crude oil the size of a whole state
moving this way and that in the Gulf waters, in spite of
every uncertainty about what will make landfall and when

and where, and no end in sight to the gushing from a deep and open wound in the ocean's floor. Unless you have a particular job to do in the repair and you know what that is, and maybe even then, especially even then, open your throat and sing, loved ones, sing!

Yours in the garden,

of the garden,

for the garden,

Susan/Shoshana Asiel

I am thinking it goes without saying that we should be spending as much time outdoors as possible. But I catch myself here. I know I often need reminders to do what brings me true pleasure and sustained nourishment. So let me say it boldly and without reservation: Into the garden with you, then! Go! Sing your song. Too dark or chilly for you? Go in your mind, then, and make a pledge to yourself to go when you can.

Day 40
Hod sh'b'Yesod: **Glory within Commitment**

(*Eve of the 40th day, the fifth day of the sixth week of the Omer.*)

bah'Ruch ah'Tah ahdoh'Nai, ehloh'Heynu Meh'lehch ha'oh'Lahm, ah'Shair k'd'Shahnu b'meetz'vo'Tahv, v'tzee'Vahnu Ahl s'fee'Raht hah'O'mer.

Blessed are You, God, Source of All Our Bonds,
You make us holy through Your *mitzvot*,
commanding us to count the *Omer*.

ha Yoam ar'bah'Eem Yoam, sh'Heym chah'mee'Shah

sha'voo'Oat vah'chah'mee'Shah ya'Meem lah'Omer.

Today is the fortieth day of the *Omer*, which is five
weeks and five days of the *Omer*.

Hello again, Dear One. Day forty. Ready for another
round? How is your connection to earth today? Your
feet? Do they meet the ground well? Firmly, but
without heaviness? Lightly, but with commitment?

Beloveds,

The wind is up today, whipping and whirling the May trees
here in the northwest corner of Philadelphia, the
neighborhood called, so appropriately today, Mount Airy.
It's a destabilizing, who-knows-what's-coming kind of
wind, slamming open doors, filling every room it can with
great, gusting waves.

I look over my *Omer* writings of previous years and find
this message from two years ago. We were each
shepherding different weeks of the *Omer* then. Apparently
no one had signed on to count us through the week of
Yesod. Perhaps we were still a little afraid of one another,
of what the power of a strong community of souls can do,
so we shied away from the powerful bonding energy of

Yesod. However by the sixth week, I was hooked. I felt compelled to count in community, so I spoke up mid-week, after four days of communal silence.

> Dear Ones,
>
> Early this morning I woke with an *Omer* emergency: I felt suddenly compelled to verify which day we are on. Although Wendy and I counted before bed, in the dark of the morning I didn't trust that the count was correct. No one is shepherding us this week, and maybe we have wandered off the path. Perhaps we lost a day somewhere, or perhaps, just I alone am confused and separated. Where is our shepherd? I went to my calendar and numbered all the days to find us indeed on day 40, five weeks and five days of the *Omer*, as Wendy and I had counted last night. *Hod sh'b'Yesod.* It's a gate of humble glory held within a firm foundation of relationship.
>
> That day 40 would be marked by wandering about in a mental wilderness, looking for my place on the calendar, seems appropriate, doesn't it? Something profoundly important is about to happen, I think, something new about to be received, though I don't know precisely what it is and how I will be when I have received it. I do know that I am right now in a state of fear, feeling too small (not smart enough, not organized enough, not disciplined enough, not this, not that...) for the work that I seem to be called to do, the worlds I am invited to traverse. So I decide to return to the practice of counting—a simple practice, and yet it is so easy to lose track... I ask for your support.

I am sending you this poem about a fly finding the deep cup of its orchid. It seems to capture the day for me. It is what I need to do: enter the glory and surrender; give in to what powerfully draws me.

Paphiopedilum

The outrageously
absorbing
shape of you
built to stun
and thoroughly engage
has me spinning
in splendor
I cannot comprehend.
Dropped
to a depth
I have always
longed for
I find my way
on glistening steps
through the darkness
from the bottom
of your oh
so terrestrial
well.

B' yad'cha afkid ruchi. Into your hands I commend my spirit (Ps. 31: 6).

Although I did not understand at the time, it was an act of glorious surrender and strong commitment on my part:

bursting into the container of this community with my holy confusion—perfect for the day. I am grateful to have been so well received.

And here I am still counting, still coming to you.

You are my cup, the well of sweetness into which I am drawn. And perhaps today you are in need of some protection, too, from the whirling winds. I nestle down inside you this day, gathering what I need for what I am born to do. Thank you for being what you are.

Thank you for being so splendid.

Yours with a firm commitment,

Susan/Shoshana Asiel

What wisdom do you gather from the earth texts into which you are drawn, Dear One? As I write this, I ask myself, what do I mean by "earth texts?" Well, the natural world, of course. And I did remind you to get to the garden. But what is not part of the natural world? Is there anything that can be called separate from the reality of our being? What are you studying now? What do you explore, what do you want to explore, what do you need to explore, with love and rapt attention? What secrets peek through your sacred texts?

Day 41
Yesod sh'b'Yesod: **Relationship with Commitment**

(Eve of the 41th day, the sixth day of the sixth week of the *Omer*.)

*bah'Ruch ah'Tah ahdoh'Nai, ehloh'Heynu Meh'lehch
ha'oh'Lahm, ah'Shair k'd'Shahnu b'meetz'vo'Tahv,
v'tzee'Vahnu Ahl s'fee'Raht hah'O'mer.*

> Blessed are You, God, Source of All Our Bonds,
> You make us holy through Your *mitzvot*,
> commanding us to count the *Omer*.

*ha Yoam eh'Chod v'ar'bah'Eem Yoam, sh'Heym
chah'mee'Shah sha'voo'Oat v'shee'Shah ya'Meem
lah'Omer.*

> Today is the forty-first day of the *Omer*, which is
> five weeks and six days of the *Omer*.

Dear One, when you read this, it will most likely not
be Mothers' Day, as it was for me when I wrote the
missive below. But it will more than likely be *Yesod
sh'b'Yesod*, if you are reading in proper *Omer* time.
And so I invite you to study the foundation of
relationship within which you move and grow. Take a
good long look today. Appreciate. Commit to support
and strengthen what supports and strengthens you.

Beloveds,

It's Mother's Day. Wendy and I mark more than twenty-four years of the intense, foundational commitment that is our joint motherhood. I will be easy on myself and let my words of two years ago do most of the talking. This is some of what I wrote to my sister and brother Omerians in 2008:

> Dear Ones—
>
> I seem to do better counting in community, so I sit down with you again. Thanks for your responses to my baffled, though not muffled, cry in the wilderness of yesterday. Thank you for reminding me how to keep count. I had almost but not quite noticed that each day of the week is the same inner gate—every Wednesday is *Tiferet* Day, every Thursday *Hod*, etc. Seems obvious now, but, oh well, apparently counting is trickier for me than I thought. At any rate, it seems I cannot do it without you.
>
> Today is Day 41: week six, day six of the *Omer*, which is five weeks and six days of the *Omer*. Here we are—held within the very essence of *Yesod* as we weave together our community of joy-struck souls. I am struck by the value of what we do together, the foundation we lay for lives of vision and power, lives made stronger and more resilient, happier, because we are consciously connecting, supporting, encouraging, and gently correcting one another as we go. How good it was for me to say yesterday that I had had a fitful, stirred-up 40th night and to have one of you respond that her 40th night had been similarly strange. There is comfort and courage in keeping that kind of company.

Here is my poem offering for this day:

This Thing We Do

(with homage to John Fox)

When we listen deeply, each to each
you to me and I to you

there is a bridge between us, stretched
across a glistening gorge.

The bridge itself is lovely
a slender, swaying thing

lovely as the snaking river
lovely as the reaching rock.

You and I, a river and a bridge—
that's what I mean by heaven. That's

what I've been trying to say.

Have I said it clearly enough?

I wish you an exquisitely connected, fundamentally bonded
day.

From my soul to yours,

Gently swaying,

I am

Susan/ Shoshana Asiel

What is the groundwork, Dear One, of your heaven?
What makes for joy in your life? Consider how you
might strengthen the foundation that you have already
begun to lay. If you cannot find your heaven, or any
foundation for it, if your life seems too crowded or
burdened for that sweetness, begin, now, to make
space. This is done by breathing, fully in, fully out,
wherever you are.

Day 42
Malchut sh'b'Yesod: **Surrender, with Commitment**

(Eve of the 42nd day, the seventh day of the sixth week of
the *Omer*.)

*bah'Ruch ah'Tah ahdoh'Nai, ehloh'Heynu Meh'lehch
ha'oh'Lahm, ah'Shair k'd'Shahnu b'meetz'vo'Tahv,
v'tzee'Vahnu Ahl s'fee'Raht hah'O'mer.*

> Blessed are You, God, Source of All Our Bonds,
> You make us holy through Your *mitzvot*,
> commanding us to count the *Omer*.

*ha Yoam sh'Nai'eem v'ar'bah'Eem Yoam, sh'Heym
shee'Shah sha'voo'Oat lah'Omer.*

> Today is the forty-second day of the *Omer*, which is
> six weeks of the *Omer*.

To surrender with commitment. This is an idea that intrigues me. More than that, draws me. More than that, begins to define me. More than that, is now shaping my life and this very minute changing me. Thank you for listening.

Beloveds,

Shefa tells me I should make dates to lose myself, to schedule times in my calendar for explicit permission to wander off into something or somewhere. Well, on Friday my car key must have slipped off its ring in a parking lot in a distant county while we were driving Wendy's car, and my cell phone, now full of the numbers I am used to having at my fingertips, has been missing since Friday. I would be highly *annoyed* if I hadn't given *that* up last week. Today my entire key ring with the only remaining key to my Honda Civic went missing for a good hour. I began to feel vulnerable, as if pieces of me were flying away to parts unknown, as if I were caught in the middle of a great whirl, which I suppose I am. The wind, in fact, still whips around here with an unseasonable chill, though the days are long and bright.

Did I mention that I tore the corner of my left front bumper on one of our famously narrow Philadelphia streets? While backing up to make room for an oncoming car and turning into a parking space on the right side of the street, I snagged the bumper of the car to my left. Why tiny Nippon Street is not one-way, and why I chose to drive on it, I do not understand. Sometimes the shortest route takes the longest time. What to do? In addition to the usual practical things—take car to body shop, call Honda dealer about replacing the car key, straighten up the house in search of misplaced phone—what to do with the 'me' that is so discombobulated? How many other parts, I wonder, will be blown, or ripped, away? Well, all of me I guess, in time.

But I am curious to know what is being born now. I go to my roof deck and chant our "Surrender Chant" with the tops of the swaying trees.[16] *B' yad'cha afkid ruchi.* Into Your Hands I commend my spirit, my breath. Great God, the wind is strong! I let myself whirl with the branches as I chant. That helps.

And so we bring to a close our penultimate week, winding our way closer and closer to Revelation. Here's a poem to keep you company in your whirling.

Outside the Box

> Don't try
> to fill space
> with words.
>
> Let space fill you.
>
> If you speak,
> speak only
> what the sky

wants.

You will never be wrong.

And think
of all those hues

swirling obediently

from your lips.

I don't know what's coming, but I do love the sky, the way
it lifts, inspires, changes and colors us, the way it keeps us
watching. I like the way I'm drawn to it, and I like what
happens to my mouth when I begin to kiss it, drinking in
the splendor of the air. Early morning will bring a delicate
sliver of nearly new moon over my head. I can take that
down to my toes if I remember to, ingest the light all the
way down to my roots.

So I'll keep on loving and losing myself, and I'll trust that
what is coming will be exactly what is needed for the time.
And I will keep my commitment to you, beloveds. I can do
that.

Enjoy every turning.

Until tomorrow,
Susan/Shoshana Asiel

Take a breather, Dear One. Take some to sit in silence and follow the course of your breath, with rapt attention. Set a timer if it helps. See what you find. Take note.

Week Seven: *Malchut/Shechina*
Leadership, sovereignty, integrity, indwelling presence of the divine

Day 43
Chesed sh'b'Malchut: **Love with Majesty**

(Eve of the 43rd day, the first day of the seventh week of the *Omer*.)

bah'Ruch ah'Tah ahdoh'Nai, ehloh'Heynu Meh'lehch
ha'oh'Lahm, ah'Shair k'd'Shahnu b'meetz'vo'Tahv,
v'tzee'Vahnu Ahl s'fee'Raht hah'O'mer.

> Blessed are You, God, Source of Majesty, You
> make us holy through Your *mitzvot*, commanding us
> to count the *Omer*.

Ha Yaom sh'low'Sha v'ar'bah'Eem Yoam, sh'Heym
shee'Sha sha'voo'Oat v'Yoam eh'Chod lah'Omer.

> Today is the forty-third day of the *Omer*, which
> makes six weeks and one day of the *Omer*.

Here we are, Dear One, at the base of the Tree of Life,
the gate of *Malchut/Shechina*, the roots, the energy of
manifestation. The Tree of Life is often pictured with
roots in the sky and *Malchut/Shechina* as the crown.
When we manifest the divine attributes, when the
sephirot work through us in harmonious balance, we
are Queens and Kings, true sovereigns of our nature.
Today we begin the last week that we will spend
together in this form. Let us sink down deeply to reach
both high and wide.

Beloveds,

I was shepherding *Malchut* last year. Here is what I wrote then:

> Today begins the seventh and final week of counting, and I am the shepherd of *Malchut*, the integrating week of our journey. To open this gate, I stand with Rabbi Simon Jacobson—who describes where we are now in this intricate and elegant process:
>
> > When love, discipline, compassion, endurance and humility are properly channeled into the psyche through bonding, the result is *Malchut*. Bonding nurtures us and allows our sovereignty to surface and flourish. *Malchut* is the receptivity to all the emotions that are funneled through *Yesod*.[17]
>
> *Yesod* is the trunk of the Tree of Life, the strength of all the relationships that hold us up, channeling the light we need to grow and prosper. *Malchut* is the system of roots through which earth-nourishment flows. As the two mingle we grow strong and beautiful.
>
> Rabbi Jacobsen goes on to say
>
> > *Malchut* is a sense of belonging; of knowing that you matter and that you make a difference, that you have the ability to be a… leader. It gives you independence and confidence, a feeling of certainty and authority. When a mother lovingly cradles her child in her arms and the child's eyes

meet the mother's affectionate eyes, the child receives the message, "*I am wanted and needed in this world. I have a comfortable place where I will always be loved. I have nothing to fear. I feel like royalty in my heart.*"

Today is *Chesed sh'b'Malchut*. Love within Majesty—the essential flow of kindness within true power. This is the kind of leadership that heals the world. Its power is unstoppable: the urge of the earth for its own health. Our choice is to work with it or against it. I choose with, though I have moments of terror, of walling myself in, keeping myself out, hiding away from the Awesome Presence. Here's a poem that speaks from the mouth of this gate. I wrote it, with gladness, on my way to a Jewish life, though I didn't know at the time that here is where I was heading.

Ocean's Psalm

For Phyllis Berman

Now that I know you will have me,
now that I know there is shore
open and wild enough with many roots to
        hold me,
I come to you.
I come to you weeping.
I come to you gladly.
I loose my floods in the softness of your
        deltas.
In the loveliness of your listening, I land
and spill myself utterly—
with no walls to stop me, no

glass to shatter, I come over you dancing
through supple grasses, my songs
at home in the swirl of your marshes.

Some, with the wisdom of wings,
flee the whirl of me
but you whose grace is to stay
and be changed, to you I give
all of me. To you I come
in abundance, overwhelming.

So much to receive…so much to give—how can we
contain it? This counting, this moving deliberately
through the *sephirot* day after day prepares us,
makes us ready to receive the truth of what we are.
The emotional energies of our very human beings
become, with attention, gateways for God.

This week I'll be chanting:

Ivru, ivru ba'sh'arim, panu derech ha'am.[18] Go
through, go through the gates, clear the way of the
people! (Isa. 62:10)

and continuing with the Surrender Chant:

B'yad'cha afkid ruchi. Into your hands I entrust my
spirit. (Psalm 36:40)

Today, May 11, 2010, I made my monthly pilgrimage to
visit my sister at the Jersey Shore. Last evening when I
talked with her, she begged me to let her come and live
with us. I told her that cannot be. At three this morning, I
awoke, agitated. I began a conversation with… what shall I

call it? God, for short, I guess. A Presence not I, but not other either. I jotted the words down in my bedside notebook as I heard them. God responds in italics:

> My sister wants to live with me.
> *You must give up your anxiety now.*
>
> You mean like I gave up my annoyance?
> *Yes.*
>
> How do I give up my anxiety, and what will take its place?
> *You must give your mouth to me, entirely.*
>
> My mouth?
> *Not just when you are writing poetry or speaking a poem.*
>
> Always?
> *Every day, every minute is mine to fill you with kisses.*
>
> If I let you fill me with kisses, then I will know what to do and say?
> *Try it.*

I did. It works.

Many kisses,

Shoshana Asiel

Well, that was a mouthful. I'll leave you with the kisses. Enjoy, Dear One. Enjoy.

Day 44
Gevurah sh'b'Malchut: **Discipline with Majesty**

(Eve of the 44th day, the second day of the seventh week of the *Omer*.)

*bah'Ruch ah'Tah ahdoh'Nai, ehloh'Heynu Meh'lehch
ha'oh'Lahm, ah'Shair k'd'Shahnu b'meetz'vo'Tahv,
v'tzee'Vahnu Ahl s'fee'Raht hah'O'mer.*

> Blessed are You, God, Source of Majesty, You
> make us holy through Your *mitzvot*, commanding us
> to count the *Omer*.

*Ha Yaom ar'bah'Ah v'ar'bah'Eem Yoam, sh'Heym
shee'Sha sha'voo'Oat oo'sh'Nay ya'Meem lah'Omer.*

> Today is the forty-fourth day of the *Omer*, which
> makes six weeks and two days of the *Omer*.

I have few words for this gate, Dear One—both then
and now.

Beloveds,

Gevurah sh'b'Malchut. Discipline with Majesty; Strength
within Leadership; Awe, with Vision and Power; Restraint
with Integrity. This is a no-nonsense gate. Do what you
need to do for your soul, which is precisely the same thing
you need to do for the health of the larger eco-system. Cut
away what is extra, what distracts from your essential life.

The health of your soul and the health of the earth are one.
The Queen and her subjects are united. Get to it.

The Point

Do you go to the light
when it calls you?
Are you drawn
to the point, the very tip
of the land, where the simple
vertical, line of your life
delves
into the broad horizon
in the melting sun
can you stand there
perhaps forever
alone, boatless
at the lip of the water
in the shush of the sea
(kissed and kissed)
can you let yourself be
that light
that lucent
barely uttered
word?

word
barely uttered
that lucent,
that light,
can you let yourself be

(kissed and kissed)
in the shush of the sea
at the lip of the water
alone, boatless
perhaps forever
can you stand there
in the melting sun—
into the broad horizon
delves
the vertical line of your life
of the land, where the simple
to the point, the very tip
Are you drawn
when it calls you?
Do you go to the light?

Enjoy your reflection. We need your leadership, your sovereignty, your *Malchut*.

Standing with you in the light,

I am

Shoshana Asiel

Nothing more—just this radiance, Dear One, yours to absorb and reflect.

Day 45
Tiferet sh'b'Malchut: Compassion with Majesty

(Eve of the 45th day, the third day of the seventh week of the *Omer*.)

bah'Ruch ah'Tah ahdoh'Nai, ehloh'Heynu Meh'lehch
ha'oh'Lahm, ah'Shair k'd'Shahnu b'meetz'vo'Tahv,
v'tzee'Vahnu Ahl s'fee'Raht hah'O'mer.

> Blessed are You, God, Source of Majesty, You
> make us holy through Your *mitzvot*, commanding us
> to count the *Omer*.

Ha Yaom cha'mee'Sha v'ar'bah'Eem Yoam, sh'Heym
shee'Sha sha'voo'Oat oo'sh'low'Sha ya'Meem lah'Omer.

> Today is the forty-fifth day of the *Omer*, which
> makes six weeks and three days of the *Omer*.

Silence. There's a line from the Psalms that says "For
You, silence is praise" (Psalm 65:2). I give you my
silence now, Dear One, my praise. Please take a
moment, before you begin, to listen.

Beloveds,

My writings from 2009:

> *Tiferet sh'b'Malchut.* Compassion with Dignity.
> Harmony within Majesty. The open heart of a true
> leader: she who feels deeply, with vision long and
> broad, and acts from the depths of her compassion. I
> woke up to the birds at four this morning—couldn't
> get back to sleep for their singing. The house wren,
> especially, with his insistent and melodious string of
> notes, held me. I let go of my desire for more sleep
> and surrendered to his wake-up call. I began to
> sense him inside me then—his song, my heart's
> pulse—and then the same with song sparrow,

cardinal, mourning dove. Where do I end and bird songs begin? Nowhere and everywhere: it's our Universe; we are it. Lying there in this expansive awareness, I relaxed into my wakefulness. Insidious worries about self and loved ones, thoughts that easily worm their way into my dark hours, could find no place to land in this harmonious heart. Perhaps there is an answer to all my anxieties in bird song.

Here's a poem I remember from another time when the company of birds helped me.

Spring Prayer

My brother and I in the wetlands watching
egrets, lovely in long white skirts waving.

It is evening: the six o'clock sun hovers
over the precious mud.
Our younger sister is horribly, impossibly ill
making all the colors vivid—sapphire
ripples through the emerald grass
carmine shoulders of the blackbirds flash.
They are rimmed with gold.

I want to say all will be well
but I do not know how or who will help
as we stand, my brother and I
in the salt marsh swaying
together in the same sweet breeze
that lifts the heron's wings.

All will be well. All is well, although God knows there are troubles enough to fret over. The awareness I meet in the gate of *Tiferet sh'b'Malchut* is big, beyond words. I carry it forward into the week, wishing you also an infinitely expanding heart.

And today, May 13, 2010: same feeling, same wish. Two days ago I was in the refuge where that poem began. I go to the wetlands now every time I visit my sister. This is one way I manage my anxiety: the salt marsh, absorbing and filtering pain, freshens, nourishes, and teaches me to receive as pure gift what is unavoidably mine. The wetlands are like the overarching gate of *Shechina/Malchut*: they give me wings to lift and transform whatever I bring here. I pray that we will learn to let them do their job for us expansively, all up and down our coastlines—soon.

And then there are those kisses, still with me.

And I hope with you too.

With love,
Shoshana Asiel.

Feeling kissed?

Day 46
Netzach sh'b'Malchut: Endurance, with Nobility

(Eve of the 46th day, the fourth day of the seventh week of the *Omer*)

bah'Ruch ah'Tah ahdoh'Nai, ehloh'Heynu Meh'lehch
ha'oh'Lahm, ah'Shair k'd'Shahnu b'meetz'vo'Tahv,
v'tzee'Vahnu Ahl s'fee'Raht hah'O'mer.

> Blessed are You, God, Source of Majesty, You
> make us holy through Your *mitzvot*, commanding us
> to count the *Omer*.

Ha Yaom shee'Sha v'ar'bah'Eem Yoam, sh'Heym shee'Sha
sha'voo'Oat v'ar'bah'Ah ya'Meem lah'Omer.

> Today is the forty-sixth day of the *Omer*, which
> makes six weeks and four days of the *Omer*.

Coming into *Netzach*, I am already nostalgic. I began
with *Netzach* in 2008… and fell in love with these
gates, this process. Here's a kiss and a twinkle as I
pass through once again.

Beloveds,

Before I begin, I want to tell you that I'll be away this
week, Sunday through Wednesday. My *Shavuot* will be
spent dancing, singing, and exploring spiritual practices
with Sufi friends in Columbus, Ohio. It wasn't intentional,
the timing of my retreat with the end of the *Omer*; it was
just the way things played out. Someone will post the last
two nights' messages for me, and I'll return with a message
at the end of the week. Meanwhile, I will carry on in the
usual way through the gloriously glimmering *Netzach* and
Hod.

From my 2009 *Omer* writings:

Netzach sh'b'Malchut. Perseverance with Dignity. Endurance within Leadership. The ability to set my sights on a distant star, while gathering the disparate energies of my selves, my inner and outer communities, for the long journey. To come into the true power of my leadership I must be able to recognize myself and my ways in the stars, as well as in the creatures winged, slithering, and walking, in the rocks, lichens, mosses, and other plants—in all the forms of nature. I must be able to see and to say from a knowing deep within who and what and how I am in order to know where we are going.

My confidence comes from knowing my place in the kinship of things, the pure and simple joy of that.

Sunflowers

I have seen
the shape
of my soul.

The stem
I struggle to keep straight
is a fluid thing:
the head I would hold up
has no trouble
bowing down.
And what I would keep
new and moist
shrivels
with such ease,

as if my soul enjoys
every second
of its changing form,
and hidden
in each anxious fear is
a long
mellifluous
laugh—

I have met
the shape of my soul.
What cannot be seen
is perfectly
clear.

The laughter at my core lightens the burdens,
undoes my fears. Perhaps this is the secret of
endurance. At any rate, traveling like this is more
fun than worrying, and I can dance without tiring
far longer than I can walk.

Today, May 14, 2010, turning toward *Netzach*
sh'b'Malchut:

I woke early this morning, adrenalized from a nasty dream.
4:40 AM wasn't too far away from the normal 5:10 alarm,
but really I would have liked that extra half hour of sleep...
The dream was a classic: I was in college again. There were
three projects that I had been neglecting. I thought I'd
check a deadline for something I was supposed to submit, a
proposal of some kind. When I went on the website to
check the status of my projects each had a bold black slash

through their images: CANCELLED. And I knew I wasn't going to graduate after all.

Well, it's our younger son who has the projects due and the high school graduation coming up. Am I anxious about that? Perhaps a bit. And I am about to "graduate" from a three-and-a-half-year inter-spiritual leadership program—that's why I'm going to Columbus—so maybe the dream was about that. The program has a focus on the wisdom of Jesus through the lens of the Aramaic language, and I expected that I would want to be teaching that work, but I don't seem to be moving in that direction. The work of my teacher Neil Douglas-Klotz has deeply informed my spiritual path. I have become Jewish in the midst of learning from him—in part because of it—but I want to deepen my roots with you now, to bring nourishment up from this soil. Well, I will have a sweet time swirling about with my Sufi friends anyway. I sense that this group of mostly gentiles with wide open hearts but little knowledge of Judaism needs me to be with them, as a Jew. What I've done in this training is good enough for graduation. I do know that.

So here's my early morning conversation with the Loving Presence:

> Why do you give me such dreams, waking me in the dark with anxiety shot out of the blue?
> *So that you will have the pleasure of again getting free.*

There are many things in my life undone,
half-finished, neglected, loose ends of
projects flapping in the breeze.
So?

Perhaps you are trying to remind me of
something I've forgotten?
Perhaps.

Take these *Omer* explorations, for instance,
there is so much I've neglected. I haven't
read the weekly *Torah* portion in weeks.
And I haven't explored the numbers and
their letter equivalents the way I would like
to. I love the Hebrew letters! I've hardly
talked about them at all... And I've
neglected Ezekiel— my study partner and I
met only once during these seven weeks...
and... and...
You must give up your shame too.

Oh, that. It takes a lifetime, apparently.
Umhmm.

But how will I be humble if I have no
shame?
I'll take care of that.

What about the Extractors—the ones who
steal from the depths of the earth, and heap
up riches for themselves? What about the
people who profit wildly from the
promotions of weapons big and small, and
all those who make money in ways that are

damaging to others? Shouldn't they have shame?
You are my project, my work in progress.

Me?
All of you.

Oh, you mean "them" too?
[a knowing silence]

And when I live my life as a creature of yours, as part of your creation, your "work in progress," then I am naturally humble?
Close to me, yes, very close.

Okay. I'll give up the shame then. Again.
I'll hold you to that. Count on it.

Much love,

Susan/Shoshana Asiel

Three more days of this. Do you, too, struggle? Are there voices pulling you from your path? Energies that seem to drag you down or hype you up? These too are God. Greet them as such, but remember to listen between the lines. The clearest messages come through silence, on the wings of the breath. So please, Dear One, make room for that.

Day 47
Hod she b' Malchut: **Humility, with Royalty**

(Eve of the 47th day, the fifth day of the seventh week of
the *Omer*.)

*bah'Ruch ah'Tah ahdoh'Nai, ehloh'Heynu Meh'lehch
ha'oh'Lahm, ah'Shair k'd'Shahnu b'meetz'vo'Tahv,
v'tzee'Vahnu Ahl s'fee'Raht hah'O'mer.*

> Blessed are You, God, Source of Majesty, You
> make us holy through Your *mitzvot*, commanding us
> to count the *Omer*.

*Ha Yaom sheev'Ah v'ar'bah'Eem Yoam, sh'Heym shee'Sha
sha'voo'Oat vah'cha'mee'Sha ya'Meem lah'Omer.*

> Today is the forty-seventh day of the *Omer*, which
> makes six weeks and five days of the *Omer*.

Still there? Still breathing? Listening?

Beloveds,

My message from 2009:

> *Hod sh'b'Malchut*: Glory at the root of things,
> Humility with a royal bearing, or what Rabbi
> Jacobsen calls, "the humble appreciation of an
> exceptional gift."[19] I am one of a kind, blessed with
> a thoroughly unique set of fingerprints. What do I
> use these remarkable hands to make? Whom do
> they serve? I am able to glory in my individual
> voice when, and only when, I know what my voice

is for. The gate of *Hod sh'b'Malchut* is like this orchid I met once, a fetching and shameless propagator, through the eyes and brush of painter Sara Steele.[20]

Orchid Tells All

However forwardly I face you
however unabashed I am—
these blazing hips, this
open-chested stance—
it's only half the truth.

Look behind me:
see how loosely, how
thinly tethered to the green I am—
continually stepping off my stem
into the cobalt air

where the magenta I meet
mingles with my belly's
yellow fire
and I am charged
with the task of

calling you here.
Color, shape, smell—
every wave of me works
to draw you.
Everything you do in me

will flourish.

The gate of *Hod sh'b'Malchut* whispers forcefully, "Go all out for glory! Attract to yourself what you need to be fully yourself. It's for the best." I remember a line from an old Lily Tomlin routine: "I always wanted to be somebody," the character laments wistfully. "Now I see I should have been more specific." Be specific. Give out who you really are. Let us know.

And don't forget to fall into the depths of the ones who call you along the way. That's how we'll flourish—all of us.

I have one thing to add now, in 2010: The orchid in whose voice I was writing is the *Masdevallia Veitchiana* or Devil Orchid. To attract her fly pollinator, she smells like trash. She has no shame, really.

I'm off to Columbus to pollinate now, free for the moment, of shame, arrogance, and anxiety. Betsy will post my 2009 writings as is. I'll catch up with you at the end of the week, after *Shavuot*.

See you at Sinai. Enjoy all.

With many blessings and much love,
Shoshana Asiel

I find I don't have much to say to you in these margins now, Dear One, Reader of the Present Moment. I hope you sense, in the white spaces, my deepest appreciation for your continued, and most evocative, presence.

Day 48
Yesod sh' b'Malchut: The Foundation of Majesty

(Eve of the 48th day, the sixth day of the seventh week of the *Omer*.)

bah'Ruch ah'Tah ahdoh'Nai, ehloh'Heynu Meh'lehch ha'oh'Lahm, ah'Shair k'd'Shahnu b'meetz'vo'Tahv, v'tzee'Vahnu Ahl s'fee'Raht hah'O'mer.

> Blessed are You, God, Source of Majesty, You make us holy through Your *mitzvot*, commanding us to count the *Omer*.

Ha Yaom sh'moan'Ah v'ar'bah'Eem Yoam, sh'Heym shee'Sha sha'voo'Oat v'shee'Sha ya'Meem lah'Omer.

> Today is the forty-eighth day of the *Omer*, which makes six weeks and six days of the *Omer*.

Continuing on, in gratitude…

Writings from 2009:

Beloved Wanderers—

> Tonight begins day 48, six weeks and six days of the *Omer*, the gate of *Yesod sh' b'Malchut*. We are getting to the bottom of it, the very foundation of majesty, how we are held up, supported by our

relationships, our abilities to bond. We come to know and value ourselves in relationship. There is no getting away from that. We are born into families of one kind or another, requiring intimacy to know ourselves, nourishment to grow. Our sovereignty is predicated upon how we are *in connection* to our parents and grandparents, siblings, neighbors, friends, lovers, partners, brothers, and sisters in community...

Often, in our first families, we do not get what we need in the way we need to flourish readily. Something goes wrong in the little basket of beings we are born into. We are sent down the river alone, or so it seems. We cannot seem to find our way, and we go about the world sucking up what passes for nourishment wherever we come upon it. I have lived like this, and I have had some help learning to live otherwise. I wrote this poem in my young womanhood, responding to the well-timed question of a skilled and compassionate healer.

A Different Dream

Would you like to have a different dream?
The dream that you have
all the love from your father that you want
and all the love from your mother that you
          want
the dream that you have both your mother
and your father
all you want
the dream that you don't have to choose?

The dream that your father
knows how to love you

with the full and sensitive love
of a man who loves his life
whose work
is the exact measure of his kindness
his urge to be useful
his love of people and of touch
of humor and of strong feeling
a man who dreamed
that he had the love
of both his mother and his father
all that he wanted
and so was able to love his daughter
all that he wanted
all that she wanted.

And no one was frightened
no one was scared away
not even your mother
because she also had the dream
the dream in which everyone was powerful
women too
and no one was afraid of the power of
women
no one was afraid of the power of little girls
the dream in which everyone was sexual
mothers too
everyone was in love with each other
and all they fought
was that which imprisoned them
that which kept them apart.

Would you like that dream?

Well, then, here it is.

As prophets, as speakers and singers of truth, we are
bearers of this dream, guiding ourselves and one
another toward a new territory, the promised land,
the one in which we live together in love. As
leaders, let us continue to help each other along. Let
us open our mouths and proclaim: *The dream is
real. The land is here. It belongs to all of us. Now.*

From the enduring foundation of a Great Love I am,
truly yours,
Shoshana Asiel

and yours…

Day 49
Malchut sh'b'Malchut: Surrender in Majesty

(Eve of the 49th day, the seventh day of the seventh week
of the *Omer*.)

*bah'Ruch ah'Tah ahdoh'Nai, ehloh'Heynu Meh'lehch
ha'oh'Lahm, ah'Shair k'd'Shahnu b'meetz'vo'Tahv,
v'tzee'Vahnu Ahl s'fee'Raht hah'O'mer.*

> Blessed are You, God, Source of Majesty, You
> make us holy through Your *mitzvot*, commanding us
> to count the *Omer*.

*Ha Yaom teesh'Ah v'ar'bah'Eem Yoam, sh'Heym shee'Vah
sha'voo'Oat lah'Omer.*

> Today is the forty-ninth day of the *Omer*, which
> makes seven weeks of the *Omer*.

Seven times seven. Here we are.

These are the writings from 2009:

Beloved Wanderers—

Tonight begins day 49, last day of the *Omer*, the
gate of *Malchut sh' b'Malchut*. This is the day that
will lead us to Sinai, to whatever it is that will be
revealed to us in this holy mountain, as much as we
can receive within the readiness of our time. Here,
insofar as we open, is the wholeness of our being,
the holiness of our humanity. We are fully alive
now, fully surrendered to the process of living on—
in—this earth. Here we are now arriving; in
whatever rag-tag state we may be in, coming into
our true being. Can you believe it? If you can't
quite, don't worry, we are making it anyway. Take
my word for it, if you will, or just relax into the
closing and experience the dance however you do.
These gates have wound us round and round, down
and in, up and out at once, into the very center of
our being, the place in which we are standing right
now and through which we are always moving.
Dizzying yes, but with *Malchut*, in *Malchut*, we
hold the center: our feet know the ground even as
we spin.

Here's a poem, a new one, commissioned by a
community choir for their tenth anniversary
celebration, which is coming up in June. I wrote the
choir a blessing, so that they could receive it
themselves and pass the blessing on to their
audience. The piece has been set to music by
composer Andrea Clearfield and will be sung by
full chorus, with flute, piano and vibraphone, on
June 6.[21] Perhaps you can hear some of the music as
you read…

Into the Blue: A Blessing From the
Rainbow Chorale

May you be met
at the door and greeted
by the kindest of breezes,
the kind that rises
from the earth
through the throats
of the ones who breathe
Alleluia.

May you be swept up
in the love of a song,
lean and laugh
like some lily in the wind—
there's nothing to catch us
but air,
and our stalks
strong enough to
split the earth
and reach
for the summer sun.

May you seek the green and
receive what you need:
from the light,
through the breath
that lifts us up, out of
the tangles of our roots
and around
even the most oppressive
rock.

In good, kind company
may you lengthen, swell
soften, spread,
send the colors of your voice,
every russet, carnelian,
deep yellow
stripe of your flame
into the blue
Alleluia

as a chorus of future lilies
flourishes through you

day after day
week after week
June after June
giving up, giving in, giving out:
trumpeting
the exquisite, excruciating
pleasure of
growing here.

> *Commissioned by the*
> *Rainbow Chorale of*
> *Delaware to celebrate its*
> *tenth anniversary season.*

I send it as a blessing to you also and leave you chanting: *Kamti ani lif 'toach l'dodi*. I will open to you my beloved, will you open, open to me? (Song of Songs 5:5)

Thank you for receiving these messages.

Chag Sameach,
Shoshana Asiel

Wishing you the most divine revelations, in your time, Dear One. Here's to the sweet mystery of your unfolding! Thank you for coming along with me. Thank you for breathing here. I will return with another message, after *Shavuot*. Until then, *Hineni*, Dear One. I'm here.

Afterword

At your leisure…

Thank you, thank you, thank you—a thousand thanks for being *there* to receive my *here* as I struggled and mused my way through the forty-nine gates. I'll say some specific thanks, knowing I will never get to the bottom of that well. First of all, thanks to our teacher Shefa for creating and holding the *Kol Zimra* community and for giving me the green light to write my way through in your company. Thanks to Betsy also for being my back-up message poster and always a bearer of deep support for me in my musings. Thanks to my beloved Wendy, my partner in the domestic sphere, for proofreading when the rhythm of our days allowed it (I usually regretted when it didn't) and for doing far more than your share of dishes while I ascended to my study after supper. Please send Wendy many kisses of support for tending the home fires while I wrote to you.

Thanks to my faithful readers: most especially to lynna: you met me nearly every day with your lower case 'l' and a transparency of soul that I cherish. It has been sheer delight to get to know you in this way. On the days when I didn't want to do what I had committed to do, the shimmer of your *neshema*, your soul light, pulled me through. And Sally, thank you for roaring and aching and moaning with me, and Chava, for receiving my gifts with such thanks from the very beginning that I had to believe I was giving something, and Matthew from the north country for returning my images so sweetly through your eyes. Prahaladan, thanks for responding so generously with your mystical romps. Thanks for the heartiness of your responses, and for letting me know about some of the territory I may want to explore in future years.

To those of you I've known longest and best—Sara, Pesach, Atzilah, Ariel, Mike, Jen—you each bubbled up with passion enough to let me know you were present in the pool of listeners, and that was all I needed. I love you. And there were many others, too, who periodically signaled across the waves to give me a sense of the breadth of this container. I am grateful to all of you—whether you read, saved for another day, or just watched the messages go by—thank you for being part of the community that called these writings out of me.

And to you, Dear One, if you are reading these words now, you are one of those who called them forth. I thank you. When all is said and done, I have adored writing them. And I love thinking of you there, taking them in.

As for my personal journey since I last wrote, beloveds, what shall I say? I have been to Ohio and back. I danced and partied with my Sufi friends at Sinai. We ate ice cream on *Shavuot*—it was sort of accidental, but duly noted. I took Arthur Waskow's *Seasons of Our Joy* along with me because I knew I would be called upon to teach them something about *Shavuot*, and I guessed Reb Arthur could help me. He did. I told them that in addition to a first fruits festival, *Shavuot* was a love story, the marriage of the human and the divine, and that it could be understood as a celebration of all oaths, all sacred covenants. I said that a proper honoring of covenants could, and perhaps should, include the covenant of peace between Isaac and Ishmael at the grave of their father.[22] I didn't talk about the *Omer*, fearing I would lose them in the trees, but kept that part kind of secret, sharing only with a few of my closest friends, as time allowed.

And what did I take away, what is the on-going revelation? As lynna said in one of her notes to me, "It's all about surrender isn't it? Surrender, surrender, surrender." But why do we, why must we, surrender? I asked this of the Mystery in one of my nocturnal conversations. "In order to receive the abundance of what is available to you," was the Response. And I saw how I want to measure the abundance, let it trickle into me in small doses. I think the gates, with their gradual awakenings, their slow and steady turnings and balancing/re-balancing, prepare me for a greater kind of reception. I expect each year they will open me wider.

So on the morning of my leaving Ohio, morning of first day of *Shavuot*, I looked through the beautiful book of photographs and blessings that my *Kol Zimra* friends had prepared for my convergence in 2008. I had brought it with me in order to show a friend who had asked to see. I looked at the pictures slowly, receiving the ritual again through the images, and this time also read the blessings that people wrote, words and pictures I had not fully taken in before, though I know I read them all at least once—maybe only once. There were blessings too big for me to take in at the time. I suppose we can receive only what we are prepared to receive. And that morning, taking it all in again and then again when I showed the pictures to my *oohing* and *ahhing* friends, I thought, "Wow. Look at what has happened here—look at what is possible! By a combination of heritage and natural affinity, I have worshipped with Sufis, Unitarian Universalists, and Methodists, and now I am fundamentally, foundationally, thoroughly and happily, Jewish. Yes, oh yes, yes, yes, and once again, yes! I will. I do. I choose this life.

We surrender in order to receive the abundance of love that is available to us when we allow it. We receive in order to pass on that abundance. We surrender again and again to that which is given us, and so we continue, *l'olam*, in the infinite loop of giving and receiving. It's a delightful dance, when we are open, and when we remember to keep on moving.

Here are two poems that came to me during my sixteen hours of silence in the car to and from Columbus. They may not be finished, but then—neither am I. I offer them to you.

Satisfaction

All day long my mouth is full
of the most gorgeous silence.

Nothing lingers inside me now
but the memory of Oh!
your fragrance, mingling with
my tongue.

If I say *cinnamon*
if I say *honey*
if I say *sweet cream* or
nectar of roses
I would not tell a tenth
of my delight.

I am slack-jawed, satisfied through my toes.
I spend the sweet, astonished hours still
tasting, absorbing, the miraculous,
mysterious and delicious
encounters with
you.

Allegheny Sinai

You, mountains that I move among,
with your ancient, rolling ways and
everlasting streams,
be witness to my love! Who else
could tell such a story, but you
who've given all your glory
to a wild, unfinished book?

Sweet, breathing hills,
stripped, plundered, invaded and profaned
in your secret and precious places,
may your enduring abandon be
my constant companion:
holder of my grief, container
of this holy rage, thunder
of my everlasting hope—

you, mountains that I move among
be witness to my love.

Thank you for witnessing.

Much love, many blessings,

And a big, wide welcome to the coming summer,

Susan/Shoshana Asiel

Amen… Ameyn… Ameen… it's an ancient word that seals an oath, establishes a covenant. It means, "May this be the ground we walk on, this the contract sealed." It means, "We stand together on holy ground." And we do. Thank you. Amen.

About the Photographs

Matthew van der Giessen is one of the Kol Zimra beloveds to whom I was writing in the original letters. The stunning images selected from his own collection were done so by him in direct response to my daily letters as they were posted. The conversation that grew between us through word and image delighted me then, as it does now. Matthew shares below something of himself and his process, and something about each of the photographs.

SW

The Path

I was surprised to find that the theme of the Path arises in many of the images I have contributed to Susan Windle's remarkable book of letters and poems. As we walk the body of the earth, it teaches us by the way the path forms, shaping the sinews of our beings as we meet with it. These images are offerings. They have arisen from a turn in the path, and have stopped me so that I had to take out my camera and hold that reverence of place a little longer.

Cover Photo: The Broken Path.

Twice in my life I have walked the great West Coast Trail on Vancouver Island. Over the 40 years between those two journeys, many of its forest paths have had walkways built that guide the traveler through jungles of sword ferns and mosses. But they don't last long. Trees fall, the jungle of the coastal rainforest continually grows and reclaims everything to itself. This broken boardwalk guides me to an essential practice. If I am to find the perseverance to step forward on that broken path, each step must be affirmed by a binding, a deep commitment, listening to how each step must be taken so that I may find myself across unfathomable distances to finally come home.

Week One, *Chesed*: Gifts of Love (Dornach, Switzerland)

Tucked behind the awe-inspiring architecture of the spiritual center Goetheanum, this little vineyard grows. The grapes were so full of life, ready to burst in the mouth. And if left, not taken in, they eventually wither to lay dried, desiccated. I am feeling the juice of the life awakening, once again, within my mouth.

Week Two, *Gevurah*: One Rung at a Time. (West Coast Trail, Vancouver Island, Canada)

The six- or seven-day pilgrimage through British Columbia's coastal rain forest would be challenging enough without its remarkable ladders. Worn, wet rungs lead the weary traveler slowly up, and then down. Backpacks feel heavier, feet and hands carefully find each edge of solid support. As much as the temptation is there to look up or down at the hundreds of rungs left in the journey, the next step is only now.

Week Three, *Tiferet*: Heaven on Earth. (Skyline Trail, Jasper, Alberta, Canada)

Like a day of Creation, this valley opened itself to my gaze. Mists softly caressing wild hillsides; a watercourse giving itself fully to its fate, still the home of bears, wolves, and eagles. It begs to be walked, felt, experienced fully in every bone and tissue. Primal life calling to primal life.

Week Four, *Netzach*: Compassion with Persistence. (Edmonton, Alberta, Canada)

This image was captured right outside my front door after one of many ice visitations in an especially long and cold Canadian winter. It captured the exquisite balance that can exist between beauty and danger. The shining path dazzles with its beauty. Keep your balance. Each step is the only one there is, the only thing I can humanly manage.

Week Five, *Hod*: Heaven at My Feet. (Bowen Island, British Columbia, Canada)

When I discover these places of hidden wonder I sometimes imagine myself being just the right height that such a secret cave would hold me. I think it is places such as this that sustain the world. These are the secret sources of water, the springs that quietly feed the streams, rivers, and oceans of life.

Week Six, *Yesod*: The Foundation of Glory. (Brisbane, Australia)

Mangrove trees, rooted like elephants standing in the mud by the river. I found these trees by a walkway on the river through the city, an area profoundly flooded not too long after my visit. The floods come and go, but the mangroves are there, still in their place. There is a deep and ancient strength that is palpable in the mangroves, perhaps because they are so solidly committed to contributing their place to the world.

Week Seven, *Malchut*: Inpouring (West Coast Trail, Vancouver Island, Canada)

On a long stretch of beach hiking, this cave-like opening had been carved through a promontory of rock. At high tide it would be filled with the roll of waves and tide, but just then it appeared as a passage into another world, the filling of our vessel as the darkness of the Great Void begins to receive the light.

Final Image: A Gathering of Stones. (Jasper National Park, Canada)

They gather by the water, solid as the mountains that birthed them. They lean on each other, commune, speaking so slow it is silence.

It is my experience that the journey of deepening into this world opens to us through image and sensation. I have found my place on that path as a clinical somatic practitioner, educator, and writer. Like Susan, I am also a student of Rabbi Shefa Gold and have found immeasurable richness in my journeys in the world of Hebrew Sacred Chant. You can find more about my work at **www.somaticsinstitute.com**.

Matthew van der Giessen

Works Cited

Clearfield, Andrea. *Andrea Clearfield Composer*. 2009.
    Web. 3 Mar. 2012.
    <http://www.andreaclearfield.com/works/choral/int
    o-the-blue/>

Douglas-Klotz, Neil. *Prayers of the Cosmos: Meditations
    on the Aramaic Work of Jesus*. New York:
    HarperCollins, 1990. Print.

Douglas-Klotz Neil. *The Hidden Gospel: Decoding the
    Spiritual Message of the Aramaic Jesus*. Wheaton,
    IL: Theosophical Publishing House, 1999. Print.

Hoffman, Edward. *The Way of Splendor: Jewish Mysticism
    and Modern Psychology* (Updated 25th Anniversary
    ed.). Lanham, MD: Bowman & Littlefield, 2007.
    Print.

Jacobson, Simon. *A Spiritual Guide to Counting the Omer:
    Forty-Nine Steps to Personal Refinement According
    to the Jewish Tradition*. New York, NY: Vaad
    Hanachos Hatmimim, 1996. Print.

Kantrowitz, Min. *Counting the Omer: A Kabbalastic
    Meditation Guide*. Santa Fe: Gaon, 2010. Print.

Mason, Ellen Ford and Susan Windle. *Already Near You:
    Poetry in Concert*. USA: Xlibris: 2002. Print.

Gold, Shefa. *Rabbi Shefa Gold & C-DEEP*. Center for Devotional Energy and Ecstatic Practice, 2012. Web. 3 Mar. 2012. <http://rabbishefagold.com/>

Tanakh, the Holy Scriptures: The New JPS Translation According to the Traditional Hebrew Text. Philadelphia; Jerusalem: The Jewish Publication Society, 1985. Print.

Waskow, Arthur I. *Seasons of our Joy: A Handbook of Jewish Festivals*. Toronto, New York: Bantam, 1982. Print.

Windle, Susan. *Susan Windle: Poem Prints*. 2012. Web. 3 Mar. 2012. <http://susanwindle.com/poemprints/?c=2>

Bibliography

Douglas-Klotz, Neil. *Original Prayer Teachings and Meditations on the Aramaic Words of Jesus*. Sounds True, 2000. CD.

Douglas-Klotz, Neil, comp. and trans. *Sacred Middle Eastern Writings from the Goddess through the Sufis*. New York: HarperCollins, 1995. Print.

Gold, Shefa. *In the Fever of Love: An Illumination of the Song of Songs*. Teaneck, NJ: Ben Yehuda Press, 2009. Print.

Gold, Shefa. *Torah Journeys: The Inner Path to the Promised Land*. Teaneck, NJ: Ben Yehuda Press, 2006. Print.

Hellner-Eshed, Melila. *A River Flows from Eden: The Language of Mystical Experience in the Zohar*. Stanford, CA: Stanford University, 2009. Print.

Levy, Yael. *Counting the Omer: A Journey through the Wilderness*. Philadelphia: Mishkan Shalom, 2011. Print.

Matt, Daniel C. *The Essential Kabbalah: The Heart of Jewish Mysticism*. New York: HarperCollins, 1996. Print.

Notes

[6] <http://www.rabbishefagold.com/TefillinPractice.html>

[7] <http://www.rabbishefagold.com/SweetasHoney.html>

[8] *Tanakh, the Holy Scriptures: The New JPS Translation According to the Traditional Hebrew Text* (Philadelphia; Jerusalem, 1985) 895.

[9] Ellen Ford Mason, Susan Windle, *Already Near You: Poetry in Concert* (USA: Xlibris, 2002) 51.

[10] <http://www.rabbishefagold.com/ExpandingInnerSpace.html>

[11] Neil Douglas-Klotz, *The Hidden Gospel: Decoding the Spiritual Message of the Aramaic Jesus* (Wheaton, IL: Theosophical Publishing House, 1999) 83-96.

[12] <http://www.rabbishefagold.com/Kedoshim.html>

[13] Waskow 178-179.

[14] <http://www.rabbishefagold.com/Opening.html>

[15] <http://www.rabbishefagold.com/Unifying.html>

[16] <http://www.rabbishefagold.com/Surrender.html>

[17] Jacobson, Week Seven: *Malchut*.

[18] <http://www.rabbishefagold.com/Ivru.html>

[19] Jacobson.

[20] <http://www.susanwindle.com/poemprints/?c=2>

[21] <http://www.andreaclearfield.com/works/choral/into-the-blue/>

[22] Waskow 185-203

18868301R00142

Made in the USA
Charleston, SC
25 April 2013